ADVANCE PRAISE FOR

BEGIN WITH WE

"McDowell has created a framework that allows everyone on the team to come as they are and deliver their best work. His candid approach is refreshing and speaks to the hearts and minds of all leaders. *Begin With WE* uses vivid storytelling and real-life examples to inspire leaders to be their best."

—**Harry Kraemer,** Professor of Leadership at the Kellogg School of Management at Northwestern University and former Chairman and CEO of Baxter International

"In both business and sports, exceptional results are only delivered via exceptional teams. *Begin With WE* cracks the code for leaders to deliver both. Kyle's guiding principles apply from the ballpark to the office park."

—**Kevin Kiermaier,** MLB outfielder, three-time Rawlings Gold Glove Award winner, one-time Platinum Glove Award winner

"Whether you're an athlete, coach, intern, or CEO, *Begin With WE* is a must-read for anyone looking to build a high performing team and inspire others to deliver at their highest potential."

—**Monte Kiffin,** NFL Coaching Legend

"*Begin With WE* recognizes the impact of starting 'behind the curtain,' developing a standard for all leaders to follow. McDowell masterfully created an environment where each team member aspired to deliver their best and worked with a purpose greater than themselves. The 10 WEs were the foundation for that success."

—**Tom Romeo,** President and General Manager
(retired) of Maximus Federal

"McDowell leverages his unique background and cultural transformation experiences at some of the biggest companies in the world to deliver insight that is lost on so many of today's leaders. The right book at the right time."

—**Philip Stutts,** Founder and CEO of Win BIG Media

BEGIN WITH

WE

10 PRINCIPLES *for* BUILDING *and* SUSTAINING *a* CULTURE *of* EXCELLENCE

KYLE McDOWELL

LIONCREST
PUBLISHING

BEGIN WITH WE
10 Principles for Building and Sustaining a Culture of Excellence

ISBN   978-1-5445-2991-2   *Hardcover*
      978-1-5445-2990-5   *Paperback*
      978-1-5445-2989-9   *Ebook*
      978-1-5445-2992-9   *Audiobook*

*To my parents, Don and Jody Jenkins, who inspired
me with their incredible work ethic.*

—K. M.

"

It is not the critic who counts; not the man who points out how the strong man stumbles, or where the doer of deeds could have done them better. The credit belongs to the man who is actually in the arena, whose face is marred by dust and sweat and blood; who strives valiantly; who errs, who comes short again and again, because there is no effort without error and shortcoming; but who does actually strive to do the deeds; who knows great enthusiasms, the great devotions; who spends himself in a worthy cause; who at the best knows in the end the triumph of high achievement, and who at the worst, if he fails, at least fails while daring greatly, so that his place shall never be with those cold and timid souls who neither know victory nor defeat.

"

—THEODORE ROOSEVELT, "CITIZENSHIP IN A REPUBLIC,"
DELIVERED AT THE SORBONNE, IN PARIS, FRANCE, ON APRIL 23, 1910

CONTENTS

INTRODUCTION

It was midnight in Lawrence, Kansas. Still wearing that day's suit, I stared at my laptop in the dark hotel room. It had been three months since I began my role as Senior Vice President and Program Manager at Maximus, one of the largest business process outsourcing firms in the country. The next day, I would be speaking to the top fifty leaders of my newly inherited contact center program: a team of highly talented men and women who lead more than fourteen thousand customer service professionals in the largest, and arguably most visible, program in the Federal Government. When I accepted the role, I was given two primary objectives, and my charter was simple: lead a sorely needed cultural transformation and, quite simply, help the program be better across the board. Tomorrow was my first chance to make that all-important first impression and set the tone for our journey.

I knew there was a need for a major cultural shift. In the three months leading up to the meeting in Lawrence, I had learned there was very little shared trust among leaders. My predecessor had been known for "talking the talk" but not actually walking the walk. There was a general emphasis on what I would describe as "silo success," where each leader's focus was limited to the success of their respective business unit—rather than a focus on the macro program at large. I'd been told the operation needed to be more efficient and quality was "stale." A few of those silos desperately needed improvement, and my boss had already identified a few leaders who "needed to go." I'd also heard complaints about the level of risk-*in*tolerance. I'd come to understand there was a lot of talent on the team, but leaders seemed to be gun-shy. As odd as this may sound, I sensed the team was discouraged from actually thinking strategically—which only fortified the silos.

In terms of leading a cultural transformation, this wasn't my first rodeo. Throughout my career, I've been fortunate to lead organizations with tens of thousands of employees, and multi-billion-dollar budgets, for some of the biggest companies in the world, including CVS Caremark and Optum. Still, every organization is different, and I wondered about the right approach for this particular set of leaders.

As I stared at the blank document on my screen, I pondered the best way to pitch my message, gain alignment, and put the wheels in motion. I could get on stage and try to use charisma to win them over. I could talk metrics and objectives. I could dazzle them with a parade of classic corporate clichés—something like, "Let's grab the low-hanging fruit while we push the envelope, because failure is not an option," before closing cheerfully with, "My door is always open." We've all heard this hollow "rah-rah" language before. But given what this team had experienced from previous leadership and a challenging client, I knew these approaches would be received with skepticism at best. To them, I may as well be just another starched shirt making empty promises about what *I* was going to do and how *I* was here to save them.

I wanted buy-in, *now*. But I didn't just want blind loyalty because I was the new boss. I wanted a sincere connection with every single person in the room. Whatever the approach, I would not allow any ambiguity about the road ahead. If we were going to transform the culture of this $5 billion program, I had to ensure this group of leaders had laser clarity on my expectations. And perhaps more importantly, I wanted them to be keenly aware that *they* were obligated to hold me accountable to the same standards.

The clock raced past 1:00 a.m. Then 2:00 a.m., and I was still without any content to convey my commitment in a meaningful way. Finally, it was close to three o'clock in the morning when I realized I had something I could share with passion and authenticity. It was direct and reflected the same optimism I carried every single day of those first three months.

My laptop, now staring back at me, displayed ten items. With no intention or preplanning, they all began with the word *We*. And at that moment it occurred to me, these would be the guiding principles needed to establish our Culture of Excellence.

The next morning, I took the stage and looked out at those leaders. "I'll cut right to the chase," I said. "This team has built a tremendous legacy, and you should be very, very proud of what this program has accomplished. But there are a number of factors that threaten that legacy and the stability of our organization's future. We've got to capitalize on what's historically made you great and overhaul the rest. But how?" I asked.

"I won't stand here and pretend to have all the answers, because I don't. However, make no mistake, I am here to win! And my approach is probably different than what you've experienced prior to me joining. But I'm not naive enough to think I can make a lot of progress on my own. *I need you.*"

I turned toward the projector screen, and with a click of a mouse, the title slide created only hours earlier displayed just three words, "The 10 WEs," with its black background and oversized white font. I turned back to the team and said, "*This* is how we get there—these are our 'rules of the road.' I have ten guiding principles to share with you today, and these will be *our* guiding principles. These are my expectations of *you*." I paused. "But more importantly, these are the same expectations you must hold of *me*."

As I looked across the audience, I saw reactions of optimism, confusion, and what even appeared to be disdain. Undeterred, I added, "If you're not on board with any one of these principles, you're probably in the wrong place. They are nonnegotiable. The 10 WEs govern how we treat each other and those we serve—in that order."

The 10 WEs govern how we treat each other and those we serve—in that order.

I continued, "You may have noticed a lack of bright colors and shiny objects on the screen." I advanced the presentation to the first principle and said, "This entire presentation is black and white, because this *is* black and white; there are no shades of gray. You're in...or you're out." Without even a glance back to the screen, I shared the first WE:

The presentation continued, and I reviewed each principle in earnest, one by one.

I continued, "Whatever infighting you may have observed, whatever client dysfunction you may have seen, and whatever disengaged leadership you've witnessed, that all ends today. From this day forward, I want you to hold me accountable to these principles. In fact, it's your obligation to call me out if you see me break even one—because I assure you, I'll do the same to you. To be a real team, we've all got to play by the same set of rules."

By the time I had shared WE 10, those furrowed brows and looks of disdain had softened. I could feel an energy in the room—an enthusiasm I hadn't felt in the previous three months. While some in the audience continued to stare stoically, the expressions on most of the leaders' faces told me I'd hit on something powerful. The skeptic in me wondered if those responses were contrived simply to impress the new boss. Was this apparent enthusiasm simply an effort to pander to the new guy?

In the year following that presentation in Lawrence, I intentionally didn't push the 10 WEs. I wanted to gauge how authentic the reaction really was. The absolute last thing I wanted was some "unicorns-and-rainbows" mission statement that everyone knows exists but no one can recite. I refused to promote hollow words on a banner.

But I came to realize, not only were these principles being embraced, they were being evangelized! In my travels to any one of our eleven facilities, I saw leaders extolling the principles in ways designed to motivate their local crew. I saw banners, employees proudly wearing 10 WEs T-shirts, and even acrylic signs for each of the WEs. Then came 10 WEs coffee mugs and rubber bracelets—one bracelet for each WE (these too were in black and white). Although I hadn't commissioned any signage or swag, each location was leaning in to the principles in their own creative way. It was obvious these principles had taken on a life of their own. The WEs became part of our daily lexicon. For example, nearly every day, I heard leaders pushing their peers, using the preface, "We challenge each other, right?" (That also became the approach used when the team disagreed with my direction.) My weekly staff meetings transitioned from "readouts" to conversations, with leaders now comfortable weighing in on their peers' updates.

We were in the midst of a full-blown cultural transformation.

What was it about these concepts that was so powerful? What was it about these principles that inspired so many—with no direction from me—to make mugs and signs and T-shirts with the 10

WEs splashed across them? What made them significant enough to launch a twice-yearly "10 WEs Awards" ceremony to recognize team members who were "caught" making a difference by exhibiting any one of the WEs? And years later, long after my departure, why are the WEs still the cultural cornerstone for the organization?

The 10 WEs are powerful because they provide a simple, direct, relatable antidote to the leadership dysfunction that afflicts teams around the world, especially in Corporate America. And I'm certain millions are desperate for a cure.

Corporate A-*ME*-rica

Corporate America is broken.

But that's no surprise: it's made up of people who are a product of their culture.

Most of us learn from childhood that we should focus on getting the ribbon, getting a trophy, becoming the best in our area. Over and over, a focus on *me* is reinforced as we grow up. We post selfies on social media for our curated online personas, yet rarely do those posts reflect reality. We've been marketed products like the *i*Phone and the *i*Pad, and for decades, were sold the idea that absolutely anything branded with an *i* is "cool." Not so subliminally, we have learned to focus on *I*, *me*, and *my* above all. And that focus has extended to the workplace. We're selfishly focused, constantly thinking, "What do I need to do to impress my boss; how can I look better than my peers; how do I advance?" And of course, the one question most asked: "What's in it for *me*?"

The *I, me, my* focus is everywhere—and as leaders, we're a victim of that focus. But more troubling, we are also the ones who continue to perpetuate it. Like so many bosses around the world, I spent most of my twenty-eight-year career in Corporate America leaning in to that paradigm. I was wrong. But my journey has taught me: a boss and a leader are not the same thing. Not even close. A *boss* is *me*-oriented, makes demands, gives orders, and is always at the ready to play "gotcha." A *leader*, who may or may not have a fancy title, is *WE*-oriented, cares, motivates, lifts up, and inspires everyone around them to be their best. A leader *doesn't* ask, "What's in it for me?" Instead they ask, "What's in it for my team?"

> A *boss* is *me*-oriented, makes demands, gives orders, and is always at the ready to play "gotcha." A *leader*, who may or may not have a fancy title, is *WE*-oriented, cares, motivates, lifts up, and inspires everyone around them to be their best.

But most of us have only experienced that *boss*-driven culture. And as a result, the me-orientation makes sense.

I can hear you now: "Of course I'm focused on *I*...*I'm* the one getting the paycheck for *my* work, after all. I need to focus on *my* contribution—what *I* can control."

Fair enough—but individual contributions only take us so far. Whether it's Corporate America, sports, the debate team, the chess team—or hell, even the *A-Team*, success comes most reliably and consistently through the combined efforts of a group of people who care about each other and eagerly contribute to each other's and the macro team's success. No one person does it alone.

But alone is often where we find ourselves.

If you wake up every day focused on how you can impress the boss, get the next raise, get the big promotion, or just *get by*, you'll end up isolated. Sure, you might deliver great results for a period of time, but you're slowly putting yourself on an island. And like being on an island, this isolation isn't sustainable. When you inevitably make a mistake, you won't find anyone's hand extended to pick you up—after all, *you* probably haven't gone out of your way to pick anyone else up. If you experience a win, there's likely to be very few people looking to celebrate with you—unless they have to—since you haven't been eager to celebrate their wins. The *me* focus has mistakenly taught us that for someone to win, someone else must lose.

What is the result of this me-oriented atmosphere? Many companies operate in an environment that fosters insecurity and fear instead of creativity and innovation. All this noise results in us using only about half of our brainpower on what actually matters: solving problems, growing the business, and developing great leaders. When people are more concerned about preventing reputational harm than they are focused on generating game-changing ideas, the outcome is mediocrity and stifled innovation.

> **Many companies operate in an environment that fosters insecurity and fear instead of creativity and innovation.**

Not surprisingly, this also makes for dissatisfied, disengaged, apathetic employees who have absorbed the message, "Do what you're told, hit the marks on your performance evaluation, get the 2 percent raise, and clock out." Most companies have a low tolerance for risk, and a low reward proposition for risk-takers. So why rock that boat? Instead, we learn to keep our heads down and do the nine-to-five shuffle—an approach I ultimately found to be completely soul sucking.

We only have a short time on this rock, and we all want to have an impact. We want to do our best, but most corporate environments don't pull that out of us. Hell, it's rarely even encouraged! I've worked for three Fortune 10 firms, and I've lost count of the number of highly compensated "leaders" who, in an effort to keep the paychecks coming, discarded their thoughts and opinions and settled for mediocrity. They spent an inordinate amount of energy trying to stay off the boss's radar—but that heads-down approach leads to a dissatisfied and unfulfilling "job."

Me-oriented leadership fails to cultivate a culture where you can genuinely and even quantifiably improve the experience and impact of your employees and peers. You're just trying to meet the status quo, trying to not get fired.

Of course, none of this is good for the company, your crew, or you. Rather than empowering their people and facilitating the output of provocative problem solvers, bosses aspire to mold team members into people who laugh at their jokes, do what they say, and rarely, if ever, challenge with tough questions. The result? Vanilla underperformers who were once so optimistic and energized to have an impact, resolve to delivering the bare minimum, and not an iota more. They may not admit this out loud, but their performance screams it. Sound familiar?

As a result, the organization drags and the customer's experience is compromised. Turnover among the team is high because team members feel neglected and unappreciated. Up and down the corporate ladder, people come home and complain to their friends, partners, roommates, or pets, "I don't feel valued. I feel like a cog in a wheel. I wonder if _____ is hiring?"

This malaise is the root cause of the dysfunction that drives job dissatisfaction and average results (at best). And if left untreated, it ultimately impacts *all* employees, regardless of title.

And thus the cycle continues. But it doesn't have to be this way.

There Is Hope: The WE Prescription

What happens when we expand our gaze beyond ourselves? What happens when *me* is replaced with *WE*?

First, your team's performance improves. When the focus is less about *I, me, my* and is more about investing time and energy in those around you, teams become tighter, with stronger interpersonal connections and increased attention to macro-outcomes. That means the team is aligned and working toward the same mission rather than individual recognition. The team sees a direct connection between their efforts and outcomes. Would you place your bet on ten people paddling in unison in a canoe or one person paddling like hell in a kayak? The team in the canoe wins that race every time. When paddling at the same cadence, with the same level of effort, toward the same goals, it's impossible for a team to not deliver its best work. Likewise, it's impossible for results not to improve when people put aside self-centered agendas, lock arms, and unselfishly work together.

You also see higher-performing individuals. When the acceptance of mediocrity is eliminated and people feel safe to be their authentic selves, apathy is replaced with passion and purpose. Rather than competing with one another, team members rely on each other's gifts to complement their own, turning a disjointed group of people into a *real* team. When folks feel supported and have no doubt their leader has their back, they give their all.

When the acceptance of mediocrity is removed and people feel safe to be their authentic selves, apathy is replaced with passion and purpose.

A WE focus enables and demands authenticity—the single most valuable characteristic of every great leader. It recognizes no one is perfect and we need one another to do our best work. A WE focus levels the playing field among leader and team, allowing leaders and their teams to be transparent about their weaknesses while capitalizing on their strengths.

That authenticity eliminates fear, leaving employees happier and more fulfilled. We show up as our whole selves—warts and all. We feel like our ideas and efforts have the potential to have a real impact on those around us.

A WE environment turns *bosses* into *leaders*.

Although I've made a career out of driving operational efficiency and effectiveness, I find even more satisfaction investing time and care into others—bearing witness to their professional growth. Yes, KPIs matter—but they are only a reflection of performance at a moment in time. Conversely, the growth of a leader lasts a lifetime—or longer, when that leader pays it forward.

The 10 WEs eliminate corporate fear, isolation, and pretense, three words that collectively mean "corporate bullshit." The 10 WEs will dramatically impact an entire company, delivering better results and producing more engaged, authentic leaders.

I've seen it. I've lived it. These ten principles are powerful enough to change organizations and individuals' lives—so much so that I've dedicated the past year to writing a book about it, so this message can be shared as widely as possible.

So what ingredients make up the WE prescription?

The 10 WEs

The 10 WEs are not the ten commandments. Nor are they rocket science. The WEs establish a common framework and cultural currency—a currency that has the same value, whether used by the new intern or the most seasoned executive.

The 10 WEs are for every single person in an organization: no one is exempt. They're easy to remember, easy to grasp, and difficult to refute.

Simply put, The 10 WEs govern how we treat each other and those we serve.

> **WE 1: WE Do the Right Thing. Always.** The right thing isn't always easy to determine and is usually not the easiest path, but it's the *only* path to get people to rally behind you consistently and authentically. Accepting anything other than

the right thing, even once, is a slippery slope, compromising your brand and integrity.

WE 2: WE Lead by Example. Leading by example creates a standard by which the team, peers, and even the boss inherently measure themselves. Those in authority are constantly under a microscope, and others emulate their behavior, whether good or bad. Leaders must ensure their behavior is worth replicating.

WE 3: WE Say What WE're Going to Do. Then WE Do It. In any team environment, others are counting on team members to do what they say they're going to do. Building trust, from the perspective of the team and client, requires commitment and follow-through. We don't let each other down.

WE 4: WE Take Action. Taking Action and Making a Mistake Is Okay. Being Idle Is Not. Risk and innovation are key to any organization's success, which means the team must feel safe to explore new ideas. Only with that foundation of safety will the team take bold action. Mistakes will come from taking action to improve—and that's okay. Nothing comes from sitting idle. As the saying goes, "See something, *do* something."

WE 5: WE Own Our Mistakes. WE're Not Judged by Our Mistakes. WE're Judged by How Quickly WE Remedy Them. And If WE Repeat Them. If we expect team members to take action, we must also expect mistakes. Humans screw up—it's a given, so accept it. We don't accept hiding or covering them up. Mistakes are an opportunity to objectively improve. The key is to allow for mistakes, identify the correct path of remediation, and ensure the mistake occurs only once.

WE 6: WE Pick Each Other Up. The only way to ensure ownership of mistakes is to guarantee an environment of support. A team that is committed to picking each other up allows each person to feel safe to show up as their authentic self, risk boldly, engage fully, and feel connected to others on their team.

WE 7: WE Measure Ourselves by Outcomes. Not Activity. The biggest myth in Corporate America: a jam-packed calendar signifies importance and automatically equates to progress toward results. Endless meetings and other forms of bureaucratic activity only matter if we can clearly draw a line from the activity to an outcome. If an activity doesn't conspicuously contribute to an outcome, it should be questioned.

WE 8: WE Challenge Each Other. Diplomatically. Nearly all progress is the result of overcoming one or more challenges. Everyone on the team has an obligation to diplomatically challenge the status quo and one another—including the leader. Challenges must be grounded in data or experience, not opinion.

WE 9: WE Embrace Challenge. Only by embracing challenge do we foster an environment where the team pushes one another to innovate and deliver improved outcomes. To deny a challenge is to deny an opportunity for improvement. A challenge grounded in data or experience is not personal and usually comes with the intent to drive improved outcomes.

WE 10: WE Obsess Over Details. Details Matter. A Lot. A finely tuned and well-crafted work product is indicative of the care we put into our work and how much we value our brand. Obsessing over details is synonymous with obsessing over our clients' needs and wants. It's the difference between average and excellent.

> The 10 WEs establish a common framework and cultural currency. A currency that has the same value whether used by the new intern or the most seasoned executive.

Begin With WE

I've always appreciated candor, and that's how I've written this book. It's not meant to read like an MBA textbook. It's written by a real person who talks like you, acts like you, and has climbed the same corporate ladder you're on. During my leadership journey from an eighteen-year-old tucked away in a call center cubicle to leading more than thirty thousand employees collectively over the last five years, my vocabulary hasn't changed. I didn't start using fourteen-letter words and I still swear too much. That's why, in encouraging you to be an authentic leader, I've also written in my authentic voice. If I would normally say "shit"—well, you'll read the word *shit*. My goal is not to shock or offend, but to speak like one human to another.

In each chapter, I'll outline a WE principle, stress its importance, shed light on why it may not already be widespread in Corporate America, and provide you with practical strategies for implementation. You'll read real-life stories with examples of how and why the WEs are so impactful. And in some cases, cautionary tales will be shared. In the end, I'm convinced these ten guiding principles will make you a better leader, inspire those around you, and transform your organization's culture.

Admittedly and unfortunately, these principles don't work in every environment. Sometimes the "this is how we've always done it" DNA runs deep—too deep. So, as you read, you'll have to do some self-reflection, including asking yourself two tough questions:

1. Am I passionate about my team's results—enough to do the hard work to implement needed transformation?
2. Is this an environment that will actually allow me some freedom to drive change?

These are questions only you can answer—and your responses will guide your level of effort, driving change, in your current environment.

If you answered "no" to number 1, for what may be completely legitimate reasons, this book may not be for you. Leading a cultural transformation is damn hard work and can't be approached half-heartedly. And if you answered "no" to number 2 because you recognize your current environment would not welcome your embrace of the 10 WEs, it's worth considering whether this is an organization worthy of your efforts.

However, if you answered "yes" to both, you are ready to be the catalyst for change. The transformation that comes with these principles is powerful enough to convert many a skeptic—even if the initial skeptic is you. Get after it!

Ultimately, this book is for anyone who recognizes the cultural affliction plaguing the workplace and wants to *be* the cure. But it's not for the timid. It's for those who want to foster an environment of collaboration, care, and creativity. It's for leaders who want to inspire others and have an impact beyond their tenure, because a Culture of Excellence creates a ripple effect stretching beyond any one leader. And finally, this book is for those who believe leaders have the power to change lives.

This prescription is meant to heal on a deep level—a human level.

Through the teams I've been fortunate enough to lead, speaking engagements, consulting, and firsthand evangelizing of these principles, I've seen the 10 WEs transform individuals and entire teams in ways they never would've predicted. The 10 WEs have changed my life as well as the lives of so many others who were open to a different way of leading and had the courage to take action to start their journey.

How can I be sure we'll be better off? Because we'll always do the right thing and lead by example. We'll do what we say, and we'll take action. We will own our mistakes and pick each other up when one of us stumbles. We'll measure ourselves by outcomes, not activity. We'll challenge each other. We'll embrace those challenges. Of course, we will obsess over details.

And it all begins right now.

CHAPTER 1

WE

DO THE
RIGHT THING.

ALWAYS.

"
JUST THAT YOU DO THE RIGHT THING. THE REST DOESN'T MATTER.
"

—MARCUS AURELIUS

WE 1

I t comes first because it matters most: WE do the right thing. To build a Culture of Excellence, doing the right thing must serve as the foundation. This principle powerfully transforms your organization, revolutionizes your brand reputation, strengthens your team, and makes you a better leader.

If this principle isn't consistently embraced and promoted, without exception, the remaining WEs are a house of cards. Why? The cornerstone of any authentic leader and high-performing team must always start with doing what's right—for your company, your clients, and your crew.

The WEs *are* the right thing. If you're not committed to doing the right thing, even when it might be difficult or inconvenient, this book isn't for you.

On the other hand, if you *are* ready to overtly commit to doing the right thing, welcome.

One of my favorite examples of someone who is universally known for doing the right thing is former chairman and CEO of Baxter International, Harry Kraemer. Following a twenty-three-year career at the $12 billion healthcare firm, Harry parlayed his success in Corporate America into becoming a bestselling author, board member, speaker, and professor. I met Harry while earning my MBA at Northwestern's Kellogg School of Management.

In the early 2000s, under Kraemer's watch as CEO, Baxter found itself at the center of a scandal: the tragic deaths of fifty-three people in seven countries were linked to faulty dialysis machines distributed by his firm.

At the very first sign of trouble, Baxter quickly mobilized a task force to uncover what caused the deaths. After two months of recalls, research, and intensive tests, the task force determined the likely culprits: a problem within the dialysis filter and a chemical that was never meant to enter the bloodstream.

On the weekend the task force reached definitive conclusions of what caused the tragedy, a senior leader called Kraemer to give him the news. His response: "Let's make sure we do the right thing."[1]

Under his leadership, Baxter did exactly that. Kraemer avoided quietly sweeping Baxter's blame under the rug, which would have

---

1   Keith H. Hammonds, "Harry Kraemer's Moment of Truth," *Fast Company*, October 31, 2002, https://www.fastcompany.com/45545/harry-kraemers-moment-truth.

been the easiest and least disruptive thing to do. Instead, the company publicly assumed full responsibility. In addition to paying settlements to the families of the deceased, Baxter shut down the arm of the company that manufactured the filters because it couldn't be certain the product would be safe—a move that cost the company close to $200 million. To help offset the losses and in response to his and other top executives' failure to keep patients safe, Kraemer asked the company to cut their annual bonuses. He even personally visited family members of deceased patients who had died as a result of Baxter's faulty equipment.

These actions set the standard for how a corporation should own a mistake—and do the right thing. Under Kraemer's leadership, Baxter got in front of it: they didn't deny it; they made every effort to do right by the victims—and by doing the right thing in the aftermath, they ensured that it would never happen again.

However, "do the right thing" was part of Kraemer's ethos long before the disaster. In fact, during that call from the senior leader of the task force, the leader on the other end of the phone said, "I knew you would say that." Kraemer's people felt comfortable coming to him because he had already established a precedent of doing the right thing, which gave them the confidence to operate with total transparency. The company's culture had been shaped by Kraemer's leadership, which meant his team didn't flinch in addressing and owning the mistake. They explored the depth of the problem, addressed it, and brought it to their leader.

This is why "Always" is part of the first WE. As a leader of a team of any size, setting the foundation with this WE and never wavering enables easier and more efficient decision-making during turbulent times.

There were most likely people in Baxter's task force meetings who debated over how transparent they should be with the public. Maybe they even floated strategies to help deflect the blame. However, under Kraemer's watch, the only acceptable response was to take total ownership of the fatal mistakes. Anything else would have been contrary to everything for which he stands.

You see, when you do the right thing on a consistent basis with small, seemingly inconsequential decisions, your people take notice. And when you do the right thing over and over again—regardless of whether the stakes are big or small—you establish a standard of excellence, and your team will do the same. By the same token—if you've got a history of making questionable decisions or obviously *not* doing the right thing, your team and perhaps the entire company will also follow that example. Leaders have the power (and obligation) to shape the culture of everyone in their orbit. Your consistency on this front not only sets the standard for leaders around you; it defines your personal brand as a trustworthy leader.

Why Do Right?

Although it seems like it should be obvious, the right thing isn't always easy to determine. In simple terms, we could sum it up by saying the right thing follows the law and considers the needs of your company, your client, and your crew.

However, reality is complex, and identifying the right thing can be situational. Legal requirements aside, I can't spell out the right thing for every circumstance because I'm not in your shoes and I don't know what you know. However, in the second half of this chapter, I'll give you some tools and considerations to help you land on the "right thing" in any given scenario.

Is it worth the trouble, though? While taking shortcuts can at times be an enticing short-term strategy, sustained success comes from doing right. Always. The right thing sets a standard for those around you, allowing others to see your commitment as an authentic leader. And more broadly, a company that is focused on doing the right thing promotes a brand reputation that attracts and retains customers.

In some scenarios, the right thing can be the most difficult thing. It may require additional effort—more than you might think necessary. It may cost more. It may slow things down. It could even cost you some "political capital." You may even feel pressured to generate excuses or cut corners as an alternative to doing right. Most companies tend to be hyper-focused on the bottom line—so if making a few questionable moves leads to a better financial outcome, those actions can easily be rationalized.

Unfortunately, in most organizations and with most bosses, "easy" is the path most traveled.

Doing the wrong thing—or failing to do the right thing—may be easier and cheaper, but it's also toxic for everyone involved. However, doing the right thing has myriad benefits for everyone touched by the work of your organization. Here's why.

Monkey See, Monkey Do

First, *not* doing the right thing spreads like a cancer through your team. Let's say you observe a peer do something questionable, but no one calls them out for their behavior. Well, *you've* now gotten the message it's fine for you to do the same. Likewise, when your peers and direct reports see you cutting corners, they'll follow suit. Welcome to the conga line of bad actors. As long as the music keeps playing, more and more will join, more will follow. And just like that, not doing the right thing becomes a pervasive characteristic of your workplace culture.

Second, doing the right thing isn't isolated to only high-profile "life-and-death" scenarios. Leaders have hundreds of opportunities to do the right thing every single day. As the leader of an organization, if I walk through the office, head down, focused on my phone instead of the person walking toward me, and I don't say "hello" or even make eye contact—I'm wrong. A moment like that's not as trivial as you might think. I've just sent the message that I'm too important or too busy to even acknowledge a team member. I'm not doing the right thing for my team, and my bad example spreads.

However, your good example also spreads. When you consistently lead by doing the right thing, you're not only maintaining integrity and strengthening your personal brand; you're also setting a good example for others to follow. (It's no accident that the second WE of this book is "WE Lead by Example"—that's the most practical way leaders do the right thing on a day-to-day basis.)

When you do the right thing over and over, in plain sight for all to see, others follow suit. Likewise, if you require everyone to do the right thing and indiscriminately call them out when they fall short, the odds of a high-performing team increase dramatically. You strengthen trust throughout your organization and push people to work at their best.

High-integrity, authentic leaders develop a gravity that pulls people toward them. We all want to be around this type of leader. People tend to imitate what they see their leaders doing. They follow good if they see good, and they follow bad if they see bad. By committing to do the right thing, you not only evangelize this WE, but you also actually influence every other person with whom you interact.

R-E-S-P-E-C-T

It's important to understand the difference between a *boss* and a *leader*. While they may have the same title, a boss operates with an "I" mentality, whereas leaders are focused on WE. A boss and a leader have many of the same tasks, obligations, and commitments, but a boss's circle of influence is small compared to a leader's.

BOSS VS LEADER

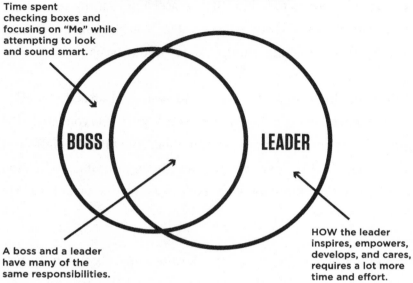

Time spent checking boxes and focusing on "Me" while attempting to look and sound smart.

BOSS

LEADER

A boss and a leader have many of the same responsibilities.

HOW the leader inspires, empowers, develops, and cares, requires a lot more time and effort.

And because their impact is a fraction of a leader's, it's no coincidence the boss's circle is smaller in this graphic. Rather than investing in their people, a boss spends much of their time checking boxes and trying to look or sound smart in front of others. If you fit this description, people may still treat you like their leader, because they have to—but all you really are to them is a boss. They don't think of you as someone they can count on for inspiration, guidance, and mentorship. No one is inspired by a boss who acts hypocritically and consistently does the wrong thing.

A leader, on the other hand, inspires, empowers, praises, critiques, coaches, develops, and *cares*. This requires much more time and effort. A leader may not even have direct reports because a title doesn't make a leader. What leaders do have though is wide influence and respect. Their selfless approach is a magnet for people who want to thrive in a Culture of Excellence.

Here's an example. Early in my tenure as a senior leader at the largest health insurer in the US, part of my onboarding involved participating in several "culture workshops," which were always led by senior executives from all areas of the company. The folks leading the workshops were essentially the face of "doing the right thing" for the company. The workshops were designed to spread messages of inclusion, integrity, service, and, of course, doing the right thing. I was thoroughly energized after each session and admired the facilitators.

In the weeks and months following my onboarding activities, I interacted with many of those facilitators on a regular basis. Unfortunately, I quickly learned many of those who were espousing a "do the right thing" culture were simply full of shit. I vividly recall a number of these people doing fantastic work "talking the talk" on stage. But not long after—even the very same day—I would bear witness to some of the most toxic, self-serving behavior imaginable. My once-high opinion of them plummeted, and I grew disillusioned about the entire organization.

On the other hand, I'll talk your ear off about some of the leaders who've inspired me by consistently doing the right thing. In fact, I led off this chapter with one, in the story about Harry Kraemer and Baxter's courage. Leaders who are guided by integrity are a force of inspiration and are widely respected. They also tend to attract like-minded people who target the same level of excellence.

Consider the legacy you want to leave behind. Do you want people to remember you as a leader who inspired them? I can attest, there is no greater compliment than a team member saying you've changed their life—that's the kind of legacy you create when you consistently do the right thing. You'll have much wider followship, with a higher degree of respect.

The Brand Element

Consumers are attracted to companies known for doing the right thing.

For instance, take the massive shift to online grocery shopping that occurred at the start of the pandemic in 2020. Like so many others, I became a major fan of the grocery delivery service, Instacart. The convenience and safety that comes from ordering groceries from home was a real game changer during "lockdown." However, I noticed Trader Joe's wasn't on Instacart—a bummer for me because I love buying from them. I couldn't help but wonder why Trader Joe's didn't offer online shopping or delivery—surely it was costing them business.

Turns out, the company didn't want to invest the money into building the technology platform required for online shopping. Instead, they wanted to invest those dollars in their employees—those who were doing the hard work of showing up during an incredibly difficult time.² Here's a quote from Matt Sloan, Trader Joe's Vice President of Marketing:

> Our main focus as a company has been *doing what's right* for our crew members and customers for decades," he states. "And in fact, it's that focus that provides the answer to one of the most frequently asked questions we're hearing right now...Creating an online shopping system for curbside pickup or the infrastructure for delivery, it's a massive undertaking," he explains. "It's something that takes months or years to plan, build and implement and it requires tremendous resources. Well, at Trader Joe's, the reality is that over the last couple of decades we've invested those resources in our people rather than build an infrastructure that eliminates the need for people. (My emphasis.)

Trader Joe's provided "thank-you" pay increases to workers, which were then doubled only months later.³ They maintained a high quality of service while taking measures to ensure a safe in-person shopping (and working) experience. And Trader Joe's is still going strong, beating other grocery retailers like Whole Foods.⁴ Most

---

2   Mike Pomranz, "Why Trader Joe's Won't Do Delivery or Pickup (Even during a Pandemic)," Food & Wine, April 28, 2020, https://www.foodandwine.com/news/trader-joes-delivery-pickup-policy.

3   City News Service, "Trader Joe's Doubles COVID-19 'Thank You' Wage to Extra $4 per Hour," Los Angeles Daily News, February 3, 2021, https://www.dailynews.com/2021/02/03/trader-joes-doubles-covid-19-thank-you-wage-to-extra-4-per-hour/.

4   Jennifer Strailey, "Has Trader Joe's Proven It Doesn't Need Digital?" Winsight Grocery Business, September 18, 2020, https://www.winsightgrocerybusiness.com/retailers/has-trader-joes-proven-it-doesnt-need-digital.

articles analyzing this surprising trend credit the success to their loyal customer base—loyalty that is, at least in part, a result of TJs reputation for doing the right thing.

Trader Joe's certainly has the resources to shift to online selling, like other grocery retailers, but the company's leaders felt the right thing to do was to invest in their employees. Some would argue that Trader Joe's is leaving money on the table by staying away from Instacart—posing a risk to the company's bottom line. But it was a move that paid off, not only with increased market share, but also strengthened customer loyalty.

There's another lesson to be learned from the Trader Joe's example. Not only did they do the right thing; they weren't bashful about sharing it. When you do the right thing, publicize it as widely as possible—especially internally among your team and company. I'm sure I wasn't the only TJ consumer who was frustrated that I couldn't use an online delivery service. But knowing *why* it was unavailable resulted in stronger loyalty from me. I saw how the company chose to take care of its people—doing the right thing.

It's not just brand reputation that's enhanced by a company-wide attitude to do the right thing; it's also product quality. Leaders who value customer loyalty put more time and effort into quality checks, taking extra steps to ensure that the product and services are fit for the public. When you care about the customer experience, customers not only see it; they'll feel it too, solidifying and even enhancing the company's reputation.

At times, you might be inclined to take shortcuts, let things slide, throw your weight around, or fail to do right in any number of ways. But that's not a long-term strategy for building a Culture of Excellence.

The Hard Part: Determining the Right Thing

By this point, you're probably saying to yourself, "Of course I want to do the right thing. But how the hell do I even know what the right thing is? It's not like the right thing comes with a helpful label or instructions." Let's break down some practical ways to lead your team confidently toward the right thing.

Like most problems or decisions in life, I've found breaking the situation down into smaller "sub-decisions" allows me to evaluate the landscape and consider potential options more objectively. I try to land on the right thing by asking myself two fundamental questions:

1. **What** is the situation I'm facing?
2. **Who** is impacted by my decision?

What Is the Problem?

The *What* question is often overcomplicated. People tend to spend unnecessary energy laboring over the symptoms or outcomes related to a scenario rather than the actual scenario itself. This is exacerbated by the urgency in most corporate environments: a fast-paced environment can cause unrelated "noise" to muddy the waters, meaning leaders can easily lose sight of the issue at hand and fail to effectively define the problem.

There are only two main actions to take surrounding the *What* question: first, clearly define the problem, including the root issue. Second, consider any ethical components.

Defining the problem is unique to your context. The nature of most problems you are trying to solve or the questions you're trying to answer are specific to you and your industry. It's not for me to provide a one-size-fits-all process to determine the right thing for every *What*.

However, there is one omnipresent element in every *What* circumstance that is not unique: scenarios that have an ethical component. In any industry and in any company, there are rules, regulations, and even laws spelled out in black and white. Doing the right thing in terms of ethical and legal responsibility is nonnegotiable. The main question here is simple: What is your ethical and/or legal *obligation* to the situation?

When someone else's behavior crosses ethical or legal boundaries, doing the right thing might mean you're responsible for calling them out. At the very least, you should distance yourself from that person. At most, you should consider distancing yourself from the organization altogether.

Easier said than done, sadly. Few people want to be the outlier, the person who's "different." If you couple that with the fear of retribution and even losing your job, it's easy to see why doing wrong happens even in companies that strive to do things the right way.

Look at the Penn State scandal that blew up in 2011. Assistant football coach Jerry Sandusky was convicted for systemic sexual abuse of several boys over more than a decade. As the case unfolded, it became clear several people knew what was happening, including head coach Joe Paterno. But for years, no one spoke out publicly. In some cases, that had to be because of fear—Penn State's a powerful football program, and Sandusky was a longtime and influential assistant coach. Anyone who spoke up could have been ignored, threatened, or possibly even fired. So many people stayed quiet because exposing the scandal posed a risk to the revenue generated by the football program as well as the entire university's reputation.

How do you think those people felt going home at night after deciding to stay silent about what they knew? How do you think they felt when the scandal blew up and the world learned they could have possibly stopped the abuse if they'd only spoken up sooner?

Making the right ethical choice may not be easy—but in the end, it's the only decision you'll be able to live with. If you need more convincing on this one, you're probably reading the wrong book because none of the other WEs matter without WE 1.

Obviously the first question of *What* is critical. But a WE-oriented leader spends most of their energy on the second question—*Who* is most impacted by the path chosen? The *Who* question can make or break your reputation as an authentic and trustworthy leader.

Who Is Impacted by My Decision?

I cannot stress enough: when wrestling with finding the right thing, clearly defining *Who* is impacted by your decision is the single most important step. For most leaders, this involves prioritizing the impact to three critical stakeholders:

1. The organization in which you function (the company)
2. The people you serve (the client)
3. Your team (the crew)

Notice there is no "me" in the list. Looking out for yourself in the decision-making process is natural—but a good leader never prioritizes "me" as it's impossible to objectively prioritize yourself among the other three groups.

Admittedly, prioritizing the three cohorts is more art than science; different scenarios warrant different priority ranking. Usually, a decision that prioritizes a single cohort at the expense of the other two is not the right one. For instance, I could give everybody on my crew 200 percent raises, which would be great for them—but is probably not the right thing for the company and wouldn't necessarily benefit the customer. Or I could give away products or services to customers. They would love it, but that would likely negatively impact the company's financials, leaving fewer dollars to allocate for the crew.

When making decisions, an ideal outcome equally *balances* the best interests for the company, client, and crew. When you do this consistently, you have a much better chance of doing right and thus, a better rationale for your decision.

In less-than-ideal situations, you're lucky to hit two out of three. This brings us to a sticky area: What happens when the needs of the company outweigh the needs of the people?

> When making decisions, an ideal outcome equally *balances* the best interests for the company, client, and crew. When you do this consistently, you have a much better chance of doing right and thus, a better rationale for your decision.

I've had to lead layoffs involving thousands of people. I've been there, and it sucks—every time. However, in a situation where layoffs are required, there are two things that provide me solace at the end of the day:

1. It's business—and, for better or worse, it's why "Company" is listed first in this filter. If it weren't for the company, there would be no client or crew. And just like everyone else in the company, I'm hired to do a job. Part of that job involves delivering in a financially responsible way for the company. If we are bloated and overstaffed, or whatever the problem might be, it's my job to correct that. This doesn't make things easier for the person on the other end, but it's a fact of business, and it's my job.

2. Sometimes it's math. For example, retail establishments must ramp up for the holiday season because the volume of sales exponentially increases. The industry hires thousands of people to handle the increased business, and once that rush is over, they have to let a bunch of people go. Keeping those employees after the holidays, when sales don't justify the additional people, would jeopardize the overall profitability of the company—the financial math makes that clear.

However, these kinds of decisions are still difficult to make when you know it's not always the most crew-friendly thing. Here's a similar example of how I've had to weigh *Who* might be impacted by a decision I needed to make.

In government contracting, there's something called the wage determination (WD). The WD is a set of wages the US Department of Labor has ruled to be the prevailing rate for a given labor category in every zip code in the country, for thousands of job types. For instance, if you're hiring a call center representative to work as a government contractor, there is a minimum amount you must pay that person, according to the WD.

In nearly all of my government work, including at Maximus, employees started with the WD for their respective role. Without fail, during every town hall or focus group, the subject of increasing pay would surface. I've been in those same cubicles, wishing I was paid more, so I understood and appreciated the sentiments I heard. And to be clear, I *could* have granted those raises—but I didn't.

Paying people the minimum? Refusing to give out raises when I had the authority to do so? How could that be the right thing? This wouldn't *seem* to be very WE-oriented.

In fact, I do believe it was the right thing. The decision was made deliberately to care for both my crew and the company. Here's why.

In the case of Maximus, I knew our operating contract would be up for rebid in a year or two. If I had given out raises, our competitors' bids would undercut my (now increased) costs by pricing labor *at* the WD, resulting in a lower bid than my increased costs. In an extremely competitive landscape, pricing can matter a lot, especially in a $5 billion contract. If our client opted to buy from our lower-cost competitor, my company would lose the contract, and my entire team—thousands of people—would lose their jobs. That's right: all those people I had just given a raise to would have lost their employment altogether.

This was a difficult situation in which prioritizing *Who* would be most impacted by my decision helped me determine the right path forward. But there's no doubt, with every scenario, every question, and every path I take, different circumstances force me to weigh the three cohorts differently.

It's beautiful to prioritize the crew cohort first, because I truly believe if we dedicate most of our energy to the team, everything else falls into place. Other times, it's appropriate to prioritize the customer. And likewise, as we've seen, there are scenarios like layoffs and salary issues when the company has to be at the forefront. The right thing is unique to every situation, but you'll help yourself identify the next best move by considering the impact to *each* of these groups.

After you've accurately identified *What* you are attempting to solve and *Who* is most impacted, make the best decision you can with the information available.

Was it the right thing? You'll know when you consult the Mirror of Truth—the final consideration when determining the right thing.

The Mirror of Truth

Your workday is over. It's time to shed the stress of the day and focus on home life. Perhaps it's time for a workout—or a drink. Maybe dinner is first on the list because you were so busy, you didn't take time for a real lunch. Maybe you chat with your spouse, or roommate, or dog (they give the best advice). At some point that evening, your mind shifts back to the controlled chaos that was your day at work.

And that's when you wonder, "Was the decision I made today total garbage? Or was it the right thing?" It's during this time of reflection that I like to have a conversation with what I call the Mirror of Truth. For me, the "Mirror" is simply a metaphor for doing some serious self-reflection.

So many of us spend our workweek on autopilot, never taking time to step away from the hamster wheel to reflect on the progress of our leadership journey and the impact we could have. However, being overt and purposeful about self-reflection is critically important.

Pick a time and place that works best for you. You might want to do it at the end of your workday when the experiences are fresh. I prefer to reflect very early, first thing in the morning after a good night's sleep. My phone is somewhere other than my clenched palm, my laptop is closed, and the world is quiet. I'm able to silence the noise, drop the bullshit, and consider, "Can I be proud of the decisions I made? What about a month from now? If it's in the press, could I defend this decision? What would my mother say?" This is my daily conversation with the Mirror of Truth.

The Mirror of Truth assigns some formality to making sure you spend deliberate time thinking about that little voice we all have in our heads or that feeling deep in our guts. I've found if the effort isn't a focused activity, much-needed introspection tends to be fleeting or simply left undone.

When I objectively inspect the image and the thoughts "staring" back at me, there are times when I mostly find solace in how I handled the previous day's events. That's confirmation the decision I made was the right one. Other times, the reflection isn't as kind. That's when I know I have work to do. (These are the days when making eye contact can be a little tough—the Mirror doesn't lie or placate). This type of self-reflection provides a genuine sense, deep down, of whether or not I've done the right thing.

Other questions to consider asking the Mirror:

- What did I do to advance my company, the client, and the crew?
- Did I make good on my commitments?
- Where did I fall short?
- Was there an obvious "loser" as a result of my decision? If so, was it avoidable?

If you've asked yourself the tough questions and objectively sought to find the answers, give the Mirror a smile and get on with your day. If the reflection isn't kind, then consider: What's the *next* right thing? What's the fastest way to get back on track? And again, get on with your day—being overly critical about a decision from the past is counterproductive.

And like that, you've just finished *inspection* of the *reflection*.

What Were You Thinking?!

The process of weighting the *Who* stakeholders is often complex— but you don't have to do it alone. When faced with tough, complex situations, I often seek counsel from my team. An authentic leader recognizes when the deck is stacked against the team, making it even more critical to share your rationale with them, even inviting them to weigh in. This allows your team to fully understand and either push back or buy into your decision; it also demonstrates that you value their input.

I've always said to others, including anyone in my organization, you may not like what I have to say, but you'll always know *why* I said it and the rationale behind my decision. I'm convinced people are much more comfortable with a dissenting approach if they are privy to the thought process that went into the decision. And my teams know they have an *obligation* to tell me when they think I'm off base. That doesn't mean they suddenly agree with me—but they're almost always less irritable once informed.

> I'm convinced people are much more comfortable with a dissenting approach if they are privy to the thought process that went into the decision.

It only takes a few instances of including the team in your thought process before this level of transparent, collaborative decision-making becomes standard operating procedure for all.

Let me tell you a story where I had to think through each aspect of the *What* and *Who* questions. Because of the enormity of the situation, I knew I didn't have all the answers and needed a lot of input from my team. And as a result of our collaboration, I still look back with confidence that we did the right thing, effectively prioritizing the company, client, and crew.

Gift Cards and Bug Spray

When Hurricane Michael hit the US in October of 2018, Maximus was in the final stages of acquiring a significant portion of the contact center portfolio from General Dynamics Information Technology (GDIT). I had already given a 10 WEs presentation to Maximus leaders, and we were in the process of weaving the principles into the program's culture. However, technically my team and I were still employees of GDIT.

One of the eleven sites in my portfolio was a sleepy beach town in the Florida Panhandle. Lynn Haven was home to about two thousand of my employees.

With 155 mile-per-hour sustained winds and gusts of more than 200 miles per hour, Michael was the strongest hurricane to ever hit Northwest Florida. Truly terrifying stuff. When the hurricane hit, the devastation left hundreds of our team members homeless and/or unaccounted for. Some had family to lean on, while others were sleeping in cars or local shelters. Sadly, many had lost everything.

I was responsible for the profit and loss of this program, but the situation was so dire, I wanted to make sure the entire company was aligned in full support for our struggling team members. This situation affected every cohort of the Who filter: there were major implications for the company, which would lose significant revenue with two thousand people offline. The customer would get shitty service. And the remaining twelve thousand customer service professionals still online would have to shoulder more of the load. And by far the most important—our crew in Lynn Haven, two thousand of our own, were in dire straits. Not only were they at risk of losing needed paychecks, but in many cases, their very survival was in peril.

My team and I brainstormed several ideas that would provide some relief, but I was looking for additional help from "corporate." I approached the division President to express how these employees were suffering. "We've got to do whatever it takes to get these folks back on their feet—my team and hundreds of employees from other locations are offering to donate vacation time so the Lynn Haven crew can get their lives in order without losing too many paychecks," I shared. I'd done some homework prior to this conversation and knew this was something GDIT had never allowed, and the likelihood of an exception was low. I felt as if this, along with other ideas, like creating a GDIT-sponsored GoFundMe, was a scenario that would check the box for the company (what company wouldn't want to be known for pulling out all the stops for its employees in a crisis?), the client (who was counting on performance from this site), and the crew (for obvious reasons).

Incredibly, every one of our ideas was thwarted. GDIT was afraid of setting a precedent they couldn't maintain. I was told, "Where would we draw the line? If we help with this situation, when will the next one come, and how much more will we be obligated?" Our lawyers even discouraged me from traveling to Lynn Haven to personally assess the situation or offer any in-person help.

At that point, I didn't particularly care about what GDIT Corporate said we could or couldn't do. I was prepared for whatever blowback might come, including to me personally. During an impromptu staff call with my direct reports, we considered several additional tactics to help the crew in Florida. Although everyone on the call knew it would be without the "blessing" from Corporate, there was no hesitation and no second-guessing. Before that call ended, one of my team members had set up a GoFundMe. (He got a call from our HR department a week later. They antagonized him for it, but I'd told him to send them to me, and I would take the heat for it...the call never came.)

We also agreed that any of us who could manage to get to Lynn Haven would do our damnedest to be there. Because of slim hotel availability and very few rental cars to be found, travel in and out of the Panhandle was difficult. Of the handful of senior leaders on my team, only a couple of us could make it work. John Hess and I made it to Lynn Haven within two days of Michael's landfall.

Growing up in Florida, I've lived through a lot of hurricanes and seen the damage firsthand. So I thought I was prepared for what I was about to see in Lynn Haven—I was wrong. Everything there was a mess. Houses were simply missing. Michael had plucked an in-ground swimming pool shell out of the ground and carried it several blocks before dropping it, upside down, in a Taco Bell parking lot.

There was damage at our facility, but not total destruction. After traversing a parking lot with too many downed trees to count, we finally made it into the office to a sight I never could've imagined: out of a crew of two thousand, a few dozen people had actually made it to work...Amazingly, they were smiling.

John and I were greeted with some of the longest, strongest hugs one could ever experience. I pulled the team into a small office, and we all just talked. I wanted to hear what they had experienced and especially what they needed. When we talked, I learned many of them had left a shelter or a neighbor's couch to come to work. I also came to learn another member of our team, Cheryl Fiala, had flown all the way from Iowa to help—she was sleeping in her rental car. Her presence was a wonderful surprise that inspired both John and me.

The stories we heard were both heartbreaking and heartwarming. John and I used the money from the GoFundMe to buy thousands of dollars' worth of gift cards. Most companies would want a strict accounting of who got what—not us. We handed out every gift card, telling the team, "This is on the honor system. If you need it, take it."

Local site leaders Marla Bruckschen and Annette Greimann were steering the ship, buying lunch meat, bread, and chips with money out of their own pockets to feed the on-site team. They each trusted I wouldn't let them go without being reimbursed. Marla's house was demolished, yet she was there, smiling and lifting spirits. Annette's home was spared, so she extended invites to anyone, including strangers, to stay at her house. Talk about doing the right thing for your crew!

Later in the day, a woman came up to me, holding back tears, and said, "Mr. McDowell, if there's one thing you could do for me...?" She went on to tell me that she hadn't been able to find any kid-friendly bug spray for her infant child. The stores that *were* open had all sold out. Her house no longer had windows, and the bugs were coming in at night; the baby was being eaten alive.

John and I went straight to the first open grocery store we could find and waited for an empty shelf to be restocked. We bought cans of bug spray and raced back to the office. She cried as I handed them over, only this time, they were tears of joy.

Sometimes, the worst of times can bring out the best in a team—making doing the right thing a no-brainer.

Leading a Culture of Excellence is easy in good times and periods of great performance. However, it's during times of chaos and uncertainty when your mettle is tested and those around you are looking at you for answers, action, and consistency.

> Leading a Culture of Excellence is easy in good times and periods of great performance. However, it's during times of chaos and uncertainty when your mettle is tested and those around you are looking at you for answers, action, and consistency.

This is why WE do the right thing. Always.

CHAPTER 2

WE
LEAD BY
EXAMPLE.

"

SETTING AN EXAMPLE IS NOT THE MAIN MEANS OF INFLUENCING OTHERS, IT IS THE ONLY MEANS.

"

—ALBERT EINSTEIN

WE 2

've always thought Michael Jordan was someone who epitomizes leading by example.

Like many basketball fans, I consider Michael Jordan to be the greatest NBA player of all time. But my reasoning isn't just about his skills or accolades. It's about how he led by example, turning around a once abysmal Chicago Bulls franchise.

In the season prior to Jordan being drafted by the Bulls in 1984, the team finished 28–54: an embarrassingly lousy record. They'd also missed the playoffs seven out of the previous eight seasons. A dynasty, they were not.

Despite Jordan winning multiple scoring titles and even a league MVP award, the Bulls still didn't win a championship during the first seven years of his time in Chicago. However, he would eventually lead the franchise to *six* NBA championships. He didn't become a champion by combining forces with other stars—the way many championships have been won during the past decade. Jordan's six rings were earned largely with the same team he was with from the day he was drafted. Modeling an insane work ethic and setting an example for his teammates, Jordan transformed the Bulls into one of the best teams in NBA history.

How that happened wasn't easy, and there's ample evidence that Jordan's approach was barbaric at times. By some accounts, his approach was downright maniacal—but it worked. He treated every practice like a game, using public criticism of the team's performance as fuel to push everyone, including himself, to improve. As a result of Jordan's obsession with excellence, other players stepped up their game and became stars in their own right. And just like a team in business, everyone benefited.

Take for instance, a player like Steve Kerr. After being drafted by the Suns, Kerr bounced around the NBA, playing for three teams in five years, before landing a spot with the Bulls. Prior to becoming a Bull, Kerr averaged an underwhelming four points a game. But following Jordan's example, he became a truly great player with an impressive NBA résumé. Kerr is now the head coach of the Golden State Warriors, so his legacy continues to grow. Would that have been possible without his time on the Bulls with Jordan?

Steve Kerr would probably say no. Here are his comments about Jordan's leadership:

He made me way better...[His message was] don't be scared. It's like, you've got to compete. That's probably the biggest thing I learned from him, watching him, was he was just so fearless. He never shied away from the stigma that would come through failure. He understood fully that if he just went all out, every single game, and went for it on every single play, the positives would outweigh the negatives, but you just to have to live with the failure...My tendency was to shy away from the big shot and just not make a mistake. I just didn't want to screw up. And so he, Michael, put so much pressure on everybody, and you just kind of realized: I've got to step up, and I've got to take my game to another level.[5]

Because of Jordan's fiercely competitive leadership, his teammates became better players. After a tough win in the early 1990s, Jordan was asked about the process and effort needed to win a championship. His reply: "Nothing of value comes without being earned. That is why great leaders are those who lead by example first. You can't demand respect because of a title or a position and expect people to follow." Jordan knew the only way he could transform his team was through leading by example.

Finally, in 1991, all the hard work paid off with an NBA championship—the first of three in a row. The 1998 season concluded with

---

5   Scott Davis, "Steve Kerr Explained How Michael Jordan Scared All His Teammates into Being Better Basketball Players," Business Insider, March 31, 2020, https://www.businessinsider.com/michael-jordan-scared-teammates-steve-kerr-better-players-2019-11.

an unprecedented second "three-peat": an amazing run of six championships in eight years.

The lesson here is clear: when you put everything you have into your leadership—your heart, your soul, your passion—and be the example you want your people to follow, you create the team you want, while inspiring those around you to be their best. It takes time, and it takes work—it's not a light switch. Leading by example means you show up every day, work your ass off, and settle for nothing less than excellence.

Leading by example while building and sustaining a Culture of Excellence creates a standard by which your team, peers, and colleagues inherently measure themselves. The leader of the team sets the bar for the caliber of work they deliver *firsthand* or cultivate from others.

> When you put everything you have into your leadership—your heart, your soul, your passion—and be the example you want your people to follow, you create the team you want, while inspiring those around you to be their best.

You Are Already Leading by Example

Fundamentally, "leading by example" means establishing a standard and following it.

Imagine your boss is late to meetings on a regular basis—not all the time, but often enough to annoy. What message does that send? That his time is more important than yours? Or he was late because he was so busy doing important *boss stuff*?

However, if your boss is consistently on time or even early? That punctuality communicates two things: your meetings are important, and *your* time is important.

A leader's example implicitly sets a standard. If you have a leader who shows up early to meetings, you feel obligated to follow suit. You make being on time for those meetings a priority—example set. Of course, the same is true for everyone who observes *your* behavior as a leader.

Leading by example requires real effort at quality control, but instead of QC for your product or service, you're doing QC on your own behavior and attitude. This includes how you carry yourself, your behavior, your choice of words, how you respond to adversity, how you rally your team to deliver—all the ways in which you engage your people.

I've even heard my *own* words repeated in the conversations among members of my teams. It's become clear to me that I overuse phrases like "unicorns-and-rainbows," "postmortem," and "Let's kill it," because I've heard those words fired back at me so often. One phrase that I'm actually proud of working into the corporate culture is, "I appreciate you." I rarely, if ever, heard anyone say it in a work setting until I started ending almost every one-on-one meeting with that phrase. I started hearing my direct reports tell their own team members the same. I also tend to hear my people swear around me a lot—probably because of my own salty mouth! This influence works both ways. My words and actions are often mirrored, so I want the mirror to reflect the best parts of me.

But the image you cast must be authentic, meaning you don't need to dress and speak like an Ivy League graduate if that isn't who you genuinely are. Your shoes don't always need to be shiny or your shirt starched to the point it doesn't need a hanger to stay upright. Authentic leadership certainly doesn't mean your words are twenty-eight letters long (although I'll personally award you bonus points if you use "antidisestablishmentarianism" in your next meeting). It doesn't mean avoiding slang or curse words and attempting to speak "perfectly" at all times. (In fact, you may have guessed by now, I happen to think some well-chosen curse words help create a more transparent, open team culture.)

Leading by example also means you behave in a way that inspires others to be their best. Work to bring *your* best, authentic self to every interaction, regardless of with whom you are interacting.

> A leader's example implicitly sets a standard.

Don't lead by being something you're not. Lead by being *you*, warts and all—and be open about those warts. People value that authenticity. Being a good leader means being relatable to those who are in your charge. It means you're clear about your expectations and standards, and you hold everyone accountable to them—including (especially) yourself.

Don't Be an Executive Seagull

We've all been witness to or heard the horror stories about how *not* to lead by example. One of my favorite examples comes from my time at Maximus. While planning one of our twice-yearly strategy meetings, a senior leader on my team shared this hard-to-believe story that occurred during a previous strategy session, several months before I joined the team.

The story: a handful of the top leaders in the organization were in a breakout session when the *boss* came in and pulled what I call the "Executive Seagull" maneuver. I'm certain you've seen this move—the executive flies in for the proverbial picnic, eats your stuff, shits everywhere, and then flies away—only the shit is disguised as "executive counsel."

He invaded that meeting, tried to sound smart, gave some directives, and made sure everyone knew he was there. That's typical enough for an Executive Seagull, but what came next was particularly ridiculous. He expressed his need for a bottled water—but he didn't just *get one* for himself. He also didn't politely *ask* someone for a water, like any normal human might.

Instead, he commented, "Oh, man. I'm really thirsty. Do I see some water over on that table? Sure would be nice to get a water over here." Subtle.

That's a full-on flex of authority. In his mind, he was *so* powerful that all he had to do was mention something he wanted, and someone would scramble to get it for him. Well, it worked; he got his water—but lost tremendous respect during this brief interaction.

And after he uttered more drivel, he left for the pool.

If you hate this guy, you're not alone. But think a level deeper into this account. Years after this unfortunate exchange, his former team members *still* talk about it—an undeniably horrible way to lead by example. The example set here was a complete focus on hierarchy, creating a Leadership Gap.

The Leadership Gap is a phenomenon in which the "boss" behaves in ways that are unacceptable for the team to behave, as if the leader has a different set of rules by which to play. The more the boss throws their weight around, the wider the gap. Case in point: Mr. Executive Seagull.

This behavior creates a gap between the boss and the team—resulting in no team at all. To bridge the gap, the boss must become a leader who leads as a member of the team—not someone sitting above the team.

> The Leadership Gap is a phenomenon in which the "boss" behaves in ways that are unacceptable for the team to behave, as if the leader has a different set of rules by which to play. The more the boss throws their weight around, the wider the gap.

It's "Me above you; you beneath me. Shit rolls downhill, so you're going to get your hands dirty for me, because I'm in charge." This focus on hierarchy dilutes the team environment and what the collective "WE" can achieve together. What's worse, this me-orientation breeds hypocrisy and discontent—both of which are replicated throughout the organization.

Unfortunately, I've seen too many bosses so entrenched in the "me," they don't even realize they're setting bad examples. Most aren't as bad as the one above, but the MO is the same: they take care of themselves first, even though it's bad for the company and certainly bad for the crew. It's what they've seen from their own bosses, and it's what they've adopted as their own leadership model. And so, the cycle repeats.

We see bad examples of leadership too much in the corporate world, and it adds up. So, what's the result of all this hypocrisy?

The Consequences of Leading by (Bad) Example

We've all heard the adage "Do as I say, not as I do." You've probably even used it yourself, especially if you're a parent. Here's the problem with that saying: in a professional setting, your every action is likely to be scrutinized and echoed by those around you. Your employees are not children, and they expect you to do more than pay lip service to doing the right thing.

"Do as I say, not as I do" is another obvious contributor to the Leadership Gap. It implies that it's okay for me to say one thing and do another—and widens the gap between "us" and "them," between "leaders" and "followers." You have explicitly set an expectation for others that you can't (or won't) deliver yourself. Would you take counseling on how to quit smoking from someone who smells like cigarettes? Or take fitness advice from someone who is morbidly obese? The gap between word and deed exposes inauthenticity.

At one point in time, I had a boss—we'll call him Patrick—who lowered his standards every time his own boss wasn't in the office. One Friday morning, while on his way out of the office for the day, he actually said to me, "When the boss is away, I *will* play." He was also known for slacking off, taking two-hour lunches just because he could. I even joined him occasionally because, at that time, I thought following this example was the best way to endear myself to him. Patrick sent the message loud and clear that what he did was fine, giving the team "permission" to take lengthy lunches too. The example had been set.

Don't be a Patrick. Leading with this type of hypocrisy derails your attempts at building a Culture of Excellence.

How?

- **Hypocrisy spreads** faster than...well, faster than you can say "get me some water." When the boss widens the Leadership Gap, the next generation of leaders follow suit—just the way I did with the extended lunches. A new boss thinks, "Now that I'm in this new position—well, holy cow, I can now behave like my boss." It's not uncommon for newly promoted bosses to assume the very same traits they loathed in their previous boss. In a nutshell, that's the perversity of "Do as I say, not as I do."

- **Inconsistent leadership weakens teams.** Let's say I have a slacker on my team, but I don't hold them accountable to the work standards I've established. I tolerate their laziness. When others on the team see inconsistency between what I say and how I manage the group, they learn they can't trust me. And it's me, not the lazy team member, who becomes the weakest link because I'm allowing something negative to pollute the rest of the organization. What's worse, my team's teams weaken because the example of inconsistent leadership sends the message that tolerating poor or uninspired performance is "okay."

- **Hypocrisy cancels loyalty.** Team building takes dedication, from both the leader and the team. Your crew won't go into the battlefield trenches with you if you're not willing to dig ditches alongside them, putting in the same amount of effort.

When a leader's actions are hypocritical and me-oriented, their negative example ripples through the organization, carrying further negativity in its wake. On the other hand, when leaders authentically uphold the standards they've set, the ripples those actions cause have a chance to be much more far-reaching and impactful.

> When a leader's actions are hypocritical and me-oriented, their negative example ripples through the organization, carrying further negativity in its wake.

Authentic Leaders Wipe the Counters

As a leader, you set an example in nearly everything you do: how you hire, how you fire, how you talk, how you treat the frontline employees, and how you treat the boss. When you lead authentically in all those areas, in such a way that your actions align with your own professed standards, your people follow the positive example.

Here's a seemingly trivial story to illustrate. Years ago, I frequently visited one of my facilities in Virginia, home to roughly two thousand incredibly dedicated service professionals. I always loved visiting this site, except for one thing: the counter in the primary men's restroom in this sprawling facility was always soaked with water. Every square inch of this high-traffic counter was wet.

Like every other gentleman who entered, I'd wash and dry my hands before exiting. I always tried my best to not add to the soaked basin. On one of these occasions, I was standing shoulder to shoulder, washing my hands alongside a member of the crew, when it hit me—so many eyes could see me contribute to the problem, but do nothing to actually *solve* the issue.

Leaders are always setting an example. Yes, even in the restroom.

So I started wiping down the counters *every time* I used that restroom. Not just a quick swipe of a paper towel either—I made sure that counter was bone-dry after washing my hands. I did this not because I'm OCD about dry countertops, but for two reasons. One, it might have made someone else's trip to the sinks less unpleasant, and two, there were always other people there, watching me doing it.

I wanted to send the message that I was willing to get my hands dirty and I care about our work environment. No one person is too important to roll up their sleeves and do something that benefits all. And wouldn't you know it, as time went on, I started noticing the counters were dry more often than not. The thirty seconds of extra effort was noticed and replicated. I led by example, and others followed suit.

Leaders who set a good example reap a host of benefits. It's not just dry countertops either; it's loyalty, high performance, better morale, more committed teams, and higher-quality, more impactful work. Leaders inspire loyalty when they live up to their own standards. People will follow you into a burning building if they see your authenticity and believe in you. Never let them question if you would do the same.

> **Leaders inspire loyalty when they live up to their own standards.**

Authentic leaders show they're human, allowing their team members to be authentically human too. They take pride in vulnerability—acknowledging when they're having a rough day, owning their mistakes, admitting they're not perfect. When the crew follows suit by opening up about their own challenges, a good leader responds with understanding and empathy.

My favorite personal example: a former colleague, John Kettering, and I worked together for fifteen years at four different companies. When I met John more than two decades ago, I was an Operations Director and he was a frontline call center representative.

It was only a matter of months before John ascended to multiple leadership roles, with the last promotion giving him responsibility for a few hundred employees. In this role, John reported directly to me. Over time, we built a relationship based on mutual respect, authenticity, and trust that benefited us both, as well as our collective teams.

John helped our teams deliver results, which often brought praise and bigger opportunities my way. As a result, nearly every time I took on a new role, including outside of our current company, John was promoted into the role I left. I won, he won—*we* won. He worked incredibly hard, always trusting his efforts would be recognized and rewarded. John went from a tiny call center cubicle to leading teams of thousands of employees around the globe.

He worked hard to never let me down—which only inspired me to do the same for him. That kind of camaraderie can't be bought, and it can't be forced—it must be earned over time through consistent positive examples in your leadership.

When leaders set a positive example, the Culture of Excellence is reflected, in part, via improved work ethic and morale. The saying "A rising tide lifts all boats" comes to mind. If the leader is truly dedicated to the team's success—both inside and outside the workplace—outsiders want to join the team. And these new members are inspired to model the observed behavior, paying it forward. If we're all following the best example, it's impossible for us *not* to deliver great results and wow the customer.

> If the leader is truly dedicated to the team's success—both in and outside of the workplace—outsiders want to join the team. And these new members are inspired to model the observed behavior, paying it forward.

Humans want to be surrounded by authentic, caring people. And this desire doesn't end when we're on the clock. So why should the workplace be any different? It shouldn't. Period. Leading by example, ensuring each team member knows their value, establishes a happier, healthier, higher-performing work environment for everyone—including you.

Practical Ways to Set a Positive Example

What does it actually *look like* to lead by example in a positive way? What are practical steps and strategies to cultivate authenticity in your leadership?

Call Out the Bullshit

There are a lot of half-truths told in Corporate America—an overwhelming amount of insincere, bureaucratic bullshit. Leaders can and should promote an authentic culture by silencing that noise and openly addressing problems head-on. We'll get into this more when we discuss WE 5: WE own our mistakes. But beyond the 10 WEs, there are ways to maintain this authenticity and lead by example.

Authenticity means what people see is what they get. If you say you're going to do something, you do it. If your corporate culture is built with a values framework, you hold people accountable to those values—especially yourself.

Here's a "Do I Lead by Example?" litmus test: if your actions were made public, would you be proud of them? Consider that discussion you had with an employee about their most recent sales call, or the way you handled a disgruntled employee, or the path you chose to overcome a challenge. If those actions were in the employee newsletter—or even in the press, for all to see—would you be embarrassed or proud? If you answered "embarrassed" to any of the questions above, you didn't lead with the right example.

Say What You Mean

Then there's the simple tactic of saying what you mean and being true to what you believe. (I also cover this in depth in WE 3: WE say what WE're going to do. Then WE do it.) I personally lean on this one often. For example, when I participate in a town hall Q and A session, I say exactly what I think—especially if the topic is uncomfortable. It's my obligation to respond with what I honestly believe and what I honestly know (confidential information aside). Sometimes the answers aren't as flattering for the company as my bosses would like, but I'm not leading authentically otherwise. If I were to reply with some "unicorns-and-rainbows" happy-talk, the audience would sense my facade and I would lose credibility.

I look at it this way: if the answer to a question is unflattering, I need to explore why. And if possible, address the root of the question.

Admittedly, saying exactly what you think takes a certain amount of confidence in yourself and your company. If you're in an environment where this is embraced, it's easier to navigate those waters. And by the way—if you *are* a leader, it's your obligation to push the culture in this direction. Ultimately, though, you *should* say what you're thinking. You *should* be your authentic self. If you come to the conclusion that you're not allowed to do this in your current position, ask yourself, "Is the money I'm making worth it? Am I really content staying with a company that won't allow me to be me?" There are no wrong answers to these two questions. You've got bills to pay, just like everyone else.

However, if you want more for yourself, I'm here to tell you, there's likely a more fulfilling work experience to be had. And if you choose authenticity over hypocrisy, guess what? You're again leading by example.

Use the Mirror of Truth

In the last chapter, I talked about how the Mirror of Truth helps leaders determine if they've done the right thing. The Mirror also helps you assess if you're leading by example. For instance, my old boss Patrick might have felt some misgivings about his long lunches if he'd looked into the Mirror of Truth. Imagine that internal conversation: "Is it the right thing to leave early or take two-hour lunches when my boss is away?" Any reflection of truth would answer that question with a resounding "no."

The Mirror of Truth can be harsh. It would be easier if an airbrush filter could be installed, but you can train yourself to welcome the truth. Push yourself to find room for improvement in your leadership. Ask yourself, "What could I have done better today?" and really *want* to know the answer.

Sometimes a trusted confidant can serve as that Mirror of Truth. Recently, I was talking with an executive coaching client of mine, Brian Alan, a COO for a manufactured housing firm. Brian and I meet once a quarter to discuss his efforts to transform his company's culture. During a recent quarterly meeting, he told me about an interaction with an executive on his team who came to him with a few questions and asked for his approval on a marketing strategy. According to Brian, he told her, "If you saw my calendar and how busy I am, you'd know I really don't have time to look at this material. Can you figure it out on your own?"

Brian told me this story in an effort to convince me that he empowers his team. However, I heard something very different than an example of an empowering leader. I said, "Brian, do you see the opportunity you missed there?" He looked at me, confused.

I laid it out for him: with his dismissal of her questions, he widened the Leadership Gap. His response implied he was too important and too busy to be bothered with her seemingly insignificant questions. What example did he set? One where leaders treat their people with disdain. Most likely, his bad example will be paid forward, and she'll treat her direct reports with a similar lack of respect when they come to her with questions. She's not going to help them—like her boss, Brian, she's likely to imply that she's too busy and too important. This is the example Brian unknowingly set.

Brian's answer *should* have been something like, "Hey, you're on the team to make these important decisions. And I trust you to make these decisions. If it bites us in the ass, we'll rally. We'll figure it out." A message like that communicates that this is a leader who cares, who trusts their employees, and is worthy of their trust in return. *This* is someone who has her back.

By the time I finished, Brian was deflated. He understood what he'd done and said, "You're right. I belittled her without even knowing it." Most conversations, big or small, can have a lasting impact on how your team sees your dedication and the example you set.

In this instance, *I* functioned as Brian's Mirror of Truth. Sometimes this is the best way to get an authentic response: go to someone other than yourself for the perspective you need.

However, if Brian, who is a good guy, were able to look in the Mirror of Truth in the moment, he probably would have seen this himself and set the right example.

It's also worth noting, many of our previous quarterly conversations were dominated by talk of Brian's overbearing and demotivating boss, Corey. Brian was unwittingly paying forward his own leader's negative example. Remember what we discussed in Chapter 1: monkey see, monkey do?

Look in the Mirror often and be real with yourself. When you put yourself in the shoes of those in your orbit, you have greater clarity about whether your example is positive or negative.

Move the Needle

Leading by example drives continuous improvement and moves the needle for your company, your client, and most of all, your crew.

Consider: How did your actions on any given day affect those around you? Did your strategies and choices genuinely further the agenda of your company and positively impact dynamics within your team? Did you inspire their growth? Did they advance your position with the client? This is the idea behind "moving the needle" in a positive direction: there should be observable advancement as a result of your leadership.

How do you know if you've moved the needle? Novel concept: just ask! Seek feedback from your employees and your clients. You can do this any number of ways; I'm a big fan of surveys, either named or anonymous. Determine a series of questions that are targeted at areas you want to improve and sprinkle in a couple areas you feel are already going well—and ask for candid feedback from your people or your clients.

For years, at many companies, I had my own direct reports fill out anonymous surveys on me specifically. I always focused the questions on my ability to execute, my ability to deliver on their behalf, and whether I set an example they were proud to follow. More recently, the survey was driven by how I do or don't "live" the 10 WEs. Without fail, some surveys came back critical, but that feedback still helped spotlight ways I could grow in my commitment to the 10 WEs and the team. Some of the negative feedback was valid, some not so much. But *all* feedback is important because it's some-one's perception. Even if I feel it's untrue, it's valid *to them*, so I need to address it. By conducting the surveys and taking the feed-back to heart, my crew saw that I was serious about upholding my responsibility to them as a leader: another example to be followed.

Align Your Team with Your Principles

When I build teams, I try to surround myself with people who are cut from the same cultural cloth as I am. Using the 10 WEs as my compass, I want to prove to others that I lead by example—so I always seek to hire people with whom those ideals also resonate. There can't be any rolling of the eyes here. We all must be on board with the same principles—no exceptions.

Now, as someone who has done his share of hiring and firing, I am only too aware that, on occasion, one of my hires might not work out. I'm not embarrassed to admit that I've made hiring mis-takes. Maybe they just weren't a good fit, or maybe they didn't live up to the 10 WEs standard. Whatever the case, it's my job to get that person off the team. Leading by example includes ensuring everyone on the team is living up to their responsibilities and their potential. If I've given someone opportunities to improve, and they haven't risen to the occasion, it sets a bad example to allow them to remain on the team. I can't settle for partial alignment—a Culture of Excellence requires wholesale alignment.

Remember, leading by example isn't just about what you do or say—it's equally about what you will and won't tolerate from your team.

Working to align your team members with your principles, and then ensuring that those principles are upheld, sets an authentic, consistent example of leadership with far-spreading impact.

> Leading by example isn't just about what you do or say—it's equally about what you will and won't tolerate on your team.

But Oh, the Pressure

Nobody's perfect. We've all got our flaws, weaknesses, and blind spots. Some days you may not want the pressure of leading by example. You may want to just hole up in your office and keep to yourself—I get it.

If you need a break, take a break—but then get back to work to make your scenario better. The more you address the challenges in your work, the less you'll experience those phone-it-in days. There will be times when you or your team might be in a tight spot and find yourselves tempted to do the wrong thing in the name of the bottom line. Don't take the bait, not even once. Instead, lead by positive example, embrace the tight spots, lock arms with your team, and remind them that together you can accomplish anything.

Not doing the right thing—always—is a slippery slope, and that's why I've already spent an entire chapter discussing WE 1. Doing wrong or slacking off—especially as a leader—is neither sustainable nor authentic. If you give yourself permission to do the wrong thing in an area that seems insignificant or inconsequential—no big deal, right? Wrong. It now becomes easier to give yourself permission to do the wrong thing for something bigger. And it's even easier for the team to stand on this slippery slope when the leader doesn't do right, setting an example for others to give themselves similar permission.

In the end, you can't possibly lead others if you can't lead yourself. Being a leader isn't about quick gratification. People will draw conclusions from observing your actions, so you're effectively creating the truth in their eyes. *You're* the standard by which everything else is measured.

> You can't possibly lead others if you can't lead yourself. *You're* the standard by which everything else is measured.

If that standard is inauthentic, or unethical, or illegal—this will be your leadership legacy and the example others follow.

Be Like Mike

You lead by example every single day. And every day, you're faced with choices: will your actions be something you'd be proud to show your friends or family? Will they stand the test of time, or will they to have a short shelf life? Your style of leadership and the way you treat others is paid forward and replicated more times than you'll ever know. Make sure your example is worth being paid forward.

Think of Michael Jordan, finally leading his beloved Bulls to three consecutive championships (twice) after years of blood, sweat, tears, and near misses. Proof that, when you put in the work and lead by example, you *and* your team win.

So, what's one of the first ways leaders positively lead by example? What does authenticity look like in the wild? How does integrity practically manifest?

WE say what we're going to do. Then WE do it.

CHAPTER 3

WE

SAY WHAT **WE**'RE
GOING TO DO.
THEN
WE DO IT.

"

DILIGENT FOLLOW-UP AND FOLLOW-THROUGH WILL SET YOU APART FROM THE CROWD AND COMMUNICATE EXCELLENCE.

"

—JOHN C. MAXWELL

WE 3

Several months ago, I remodeled my kitchen. After researching nearly every appliance manufacturer on the planet, I found a company, Dacor (the "high-end" appliance arm of Samsung), which had an all-black line of luxury "smart" appliances that were a perfect match for my overall design.

I ended up going way over budget, but when installation day rolled around, I was thrilled—the appliances looked great!

However, only days after the installation, I started having significant problems with every one of my new "luxury" appliances. The door on the refrigerator wouldn't shut. The display on the oven would randomly blink on and off—and in different fonts. The cooktop burners, which came in a cool brass finish, stained black after only one use.

And worse, every time I talked to Dacor customer service, I had to jump through hoops, answering the same questions over and over, opening new service tickets with every call. Each customer service rep told me the same thing: "Someone will get back to you in three to five days."

After several requests, I was able to convince Dacor to send a repair person to my home. I later learned Dacor policy states that before even considering a refund or replacement, a licensed repair person must visit and attempt to resolve all issues—one by one. Dacor finally sent someone to my place, a good guy who actually worked for a contractor of Samsung. Since he was a contractor, I think he felt a little more comfortable being frank about the quality of the products I'd purchased.

After about an hour of "adjustments," the exasperated repair guy told me the malfunctions were par for the course on Dacor appliances. "This is not going to get any better," he said. He also "kicked the can down the road," saying, "But I'll submit my findings to Dacor Corporate and someone will be in touch within a few days."

Nearly a full month later, after multiple phone calls to both the local contractor and Dacor, I was promised a full refund for the oven, which I appreciated. Still—even if the price was right, it left me stuck with an oven that picks and chooses when the display should be on or off.

Adding insult to injury, another month went by—and no refund. Once again, I had to wade through Dacor's customer service menu, open more tickets, and listen to more promised callbacks. I didn't get any calls. What I got were text updates every few days: "Your refund has been approved." "Your refund is being processed." "Your refund is still being processed." How long does it take to process a refund?

This horrible service experience dragged on for nearly four months—leaving me totally sour toward Dacor. And to be clear, I don't feel that way because of the malfunctioning appliances. Even with the best companies and the best products, malfunctions can happen. And these issues could've been overcome without me having to chase the manufacturer for months. It's the lack of ownership and follow-through that left me dissatisfied. Needless to say, I'll never buy from Dacor again.

I'm confident the root of my service issues weren't the customer service representatives or the repair guy. In fact, each representative was incredibly cordial and appeared genuinely interested in making the situation right. It was Dacor's operations behind the scenes. Their "service" exposed horrible handoffs and nonexistent issues tracking, to the point that it seemed like there weren't any metrics or reports to show my requests were ever outstanding. Or if they did exist, no one was managing them. The poor folks on the front line didn't know my situation; even though *I* had to call half a dozen times, every time was the first time for the rep on the other end. But their lack of follow-through indicated (to me) a failure in Dacor's commitment to customer service.

We're all consumers. We've all been disappointed or underwhelmed by bad service like my experience with Dacor. And it sucks every time.

When a company doesn't do what they say they're going to do and they fail to execute follow-through again and again, you stop buying from that company. The same is true for people. When your boss or team member consistently fails to deliver on a commitment, you stop relying on them as well. A failure to follow through causes real damage to the relationship between customer and company, as well as person to person.

> **If you want your brand to inspire trust externally, start internally with your team and establish a culture where people do what they say.**

That damage also extends to the team. When a company has these kinds of customer service issues, it's not because they *aspire* to deliver bad service or *want* to neglect their customers. It's because internally, they're not hitting their commitments to one another. That's why, if you want your brand to inspire trust externally, start internally with your team and establish a culture where people do what they say.

If you are part of a team, make no mistake, someone is counting on you for something. Likewise, you are always in need of something from a fellow team member. And it's not just your company's brand at stake—it's your own brand as well.

Why Does It Matter So Much?

Your credibility, or lack thereof, *is* your brand. It's who you are, and it's your reputation. Being a leader means serving your team and your people the way you would want to be served if you were the client: you want to be told what's going to happen; then you want it to *actually happen*. Trust sets the table for your entire operation.

Failing to deliver on a promise made to a client compromises the brand and reputation of the company. It's no different internally. When a team member commits to doing something but doesn't do it, that team member's personal brand takes a hit. As a leader, it's your responsibility to lead by example in establishing a follow-through culture—a culture that cares about each and every team member's personal brand.

When you're bad at honoring your commitments to another member of the team, it's not a leap to assume you're equally bad as it relates to your customers. Likewise (and luckily), when you're good at internal follow-through, you're much more likely to slam-dunk external follow-through with your clients.

You see, it's nearly impossible for a team of high-integrity, brand-conscious individuals to deliver bad service to its customers if they first honor their commitments to one another.

This is why we Begin With WE.

Being a leader means serving your team and your people the way you would want to be served if you were the client: you want to be told what's going to happen; then you want it to actually happen. Trust sets the table for your entire operation.

It (Really) Matters Internally

You probably recognize this scenario: at meetings, people often take on commitments or volunteer for tasks, usually with the best of intentions. However, that energy often wanes the moment the meeting ends. They forget what motivated them to make that commitment because it's not nearly as palpable as it was in the environment of the meeting, with the team around them.

Now take that loss of motivation and momentum, and pair it with ambiguous expectations and minimal follow-up from the boss. With no one looking over their shoulder, that employee is now even less motivated and less pressured to complete the task.

Then it goes south. "Oh shit, I've got this thing that I'm still supposed to do," said everyone at some point in their career. This *oh shit* moment creates a domino effect with other commitments. Welcome to occupational triage: "Well, I can move that task back because I've actually got a due date on this other one...something's got to give."

We've all been there—however, it's the leader's job to tighten up follow-through within the team. When you've got a team member who's constantly scrambling to keep up with commitments or often fails to deliver on the tasks they've been assigned, you've got a problem. Your team has a problem. Can you and the rest of the team count on this person? Are they really going to be there for you—much less a client?

No organizational culture can thrive without trust that people will do what they say they're going to do. A leader who doesn't follow through isn't doing the right thing, and they're failing to set a positive example. As renowned leadership guru John C. Maxwell said, "Diligent follow-up and follow-through will set you apart from the crowd and communicate excellence." In fact, Maxwell asserts that follow-up is a cornerstone for establishing trust. Should my team trust I'll have their back in times of trouble when I couldn't deliver on a promise when things were running smoothly? Why should they?

The most effective way to make team members feel devalued is to be absent, ignore them, or fail to follow through on commitments.

> No organizational culture can thrive without trust that people will do what they say they're going to do.

For example, let's say I have a direct report in a coaching session, and I tell him he's not quite hitting the mark in managing a strategic project with multiple moving pieces and competing priorities.

"You're right, Kyle," he says. "I have a firm grasp of our progress; it's just that I've never been very good using Microsoft Project, so it's hard for me to quantify our progress to the level of detail you'd like. Any chance I could get some formal training on Project?"

"Sure," I say. "I bet we could figure that out. Let me see what's available."

Now, if I do my job as his leader and actually get him the information he needs, then great. I'm following through, and my team member feels heard, valued, and respected. My brand is safe.

But what if I don't? What if I forget because I didn't write it down or I put it on the backburner for too long? (This is my *oh shit* moment.)

My employee feels unimportant and undervalued. It goes without saying, his project management skills won't improve. His updates will continue to fail my standards, and we'll both know it.

Trust? Gone. Leadership Gap? Widened.

My poor follow-through alienates him, compromising his and the team's effectiveness. But who was it that actually failed? Me.

In the end, failing to come through for your people creates a divide between you as their leader and your team as the subordinates. (I hate that word, but it fits here, because that's how they feel.) When you report to me, and I commit to do something for you and don't deliver, there are no concrete repercussions for me. Maybe you like me a little less, or maybe my reputation takes a hit, but otherwise, I don't face consequences.

However, when you as my subordinate commit to do something for me and don't deliver, I can fire you. That's one hell of a concrete repercussion. This kind of imbalance creates a class system and widens the Leadership Gap, sowing distrust. There are "haves" and "have-nots" now because what I'm allowed to do is different from what you're allowed to do.

That's a bullshit system, and that style of leadership is about as inauthentic as it gets.

It (Also) Matters Externally

When a company fails to deliver on its promise to you as a consumer, you receive poor service or a shoddy product. Most missteps between company and consumer are generally not intentional. But they're sloppy. And in business, "sloppy" can be fatal to the company.

If you're like me, it doesn't take much to wow you when it comes to decent customer service. My "bar" for excellent service seems to get lower and lower over time. So when a company delivers on the most basic of expectations, I'm thrilled.

When they don't, I'm not, and I'll probably express that in some way, shape, or form (like blasting my kitchen appliance manufacturer in my book). When they're upset about something, consumers become motivated to talk to other people, write reviews, or post about a product or company. Reputational damage is real and has real consequences. One review bitching about your company is an outlier; ten affect sales.

So why and how do companies get sloppy? Many times you can trace a company's external issues to internal dysfunction.

The Leadership Business

Leaders are in the service business—but a leader's primary objective isn't to serve customers. You serve your team, who ultimately serve the customer. When you make a commitment to do something for a customer, the expectation is you'll do it. Why should things be any different behind the curtain for your team members?

Here's the point: when you sign up to be a leader, your *employees* are your customers.

> When you make a commitment to do something for a customer, the expectation is you'll do it. Why should things be any different behind the curtain?

I realize this may sound like happy-talk—*oh, Kyle's gone all unicorns-and-rainbows again*—but there's a pretty solid practical element to consider. Leaders need their people to do what they've been asked and what they've agreed to do. The team is more likely to do it, and do it well, if they feel connected with their leader. More on this in a moment.

So how do you get there? First, it's important to unpack some of the basics of human nature. Ultimately, this chapter deals with the topic of motivation. You want your people to be motivated to uphold their commitments. You want them to get *why* it's important to follow through. It can't be just because you tell them it's important. By taking a closer look at those you lead and what motivates them to achieve, you're better equipped to be a leader who follows through *for* them.

We All Want to Follow Someone We Trust

Human beings are tribal. We are hardwired to work together. But given a choice, we don't want to work with just anyone. The tribe is only as strong as the trust that bonds them together.

I've already talked about the importance of leading by example—a major element required to establish yourself as a trustworthy leader. However, accountability is another important area where leaders can build or destroy trust. When leaders fail to clearly establish a system of accountability and then demand results, the ripple effect is easy to track through the company.

For instance, during my first several months at CVS, there wasn't a single meeting that passed without someone committing to doing something that they would ultimately end up not delivering. Those commitments looked and felt good, I'm sure—but more often than not, there was a failure to document the takeaway, the follow-through required, and the due date.

I didn't blame the good citizen who volunteered; I blamed the facilitator or the leader in the meeting. They've each failed to establish firm expectations. They didn't say, "Okay, great—next Monday, then, you'll have this ready," or, "Let's schedule a follow-up for tomorrow morning." Nothing. As a result, their employees offered up a bunch of smiles and head nods, but usually nothing came from this lip service. The next meeting would roll around, and most couldn't even recall what was even previously agreed to.

This phenomenon is not exclusive to CVS. If you were to keep score at your office, virtual or otherwise, I bet you couldn't go too long without at least one meeting where a commitment was made but not a shred of "what's next" was discussed. Only now, as a WE-oriented leader, you'll be inclined to speak up.

This kind of superficial happy-talk does no favors for a Culture of Excellence. Not only does it mean there's less follow-through—i.e., less shit actually getting done—but it also demoralizes employees.

For example, let's say one of my employees brings up something in a Friday meeting that sparks with me. I say, "Hey, Paul, great idea!

If you could bring that data set to the Monday meeting, we'll talk through it."

Because Paul's a good employee who wants to impress, he works his ass off over the weekend, getting that data set pulled together. Maybe he even skips his kid's soccer game to do it.

Now it's Monday, and my conversation with Paul is all but forgotten. I also forgot to write down anything about Paul's idea, so I can't even remember requesting the data set.

So I don't ask for it. And if Paul is the kind of employee who is loath to approach the boss—because, let's face it, in this kind of superficial environment, staying under the radar would be a smart move—then he killed himself all weekend for nothing. Paul goes from feeling valued and empowered to disappointed and disenfranchised.

No one wants to follow a boss like that. And you can bet a situation like this saps Paul's motivation to go above and beyond for the company. Why should he bust his ass to be an all-star employee if no one even notices? Better to keep his head down and just go through the motions.

We All Crave Consistency

Most people like guidance and love consistency. As a leader, your team depends on you for both. And when you don't bring both to the table, they lose confidence in you, and your ability to lead is compromised.

In a recent consulting engagement, Delaney, a mid-level manager, shared how proud she was of her team's commitment to on-time delivery of weekly status reports. "We used to be *all over the place*. But I set a standard that all reports need to be submitted by Monday at 9:00 a.m. I had some grumbling at first, but it's worked out great," she exclaimed gleefully. "Well, everyone except Raquel, but she's always been the late one."

Now, you might be thinking 90 percent is a pretty good success rate. On the surface, it looks like Delaney and her team are aligned on the importance of the Monday at 9:00 a.m. commitment, and maybe they are—but there is a more important element to examine. If Raquel continues to miss the deadline with no repercussions because "it's just Raquel," Delaney's sent the following message: "WE say what we're going to do. Then we do it. Well, most of us... most of the time."

The problem is, "most of the time" isn't consistent, and Delaney's opened the door for other sloppy, unmanaged behavior. Delaney *said* what they were going to do, but her lack of follow-through implies they don't all actually *need* to do it.

This is inconsistency in action and undermines every other aspect of your ability to lead. People sense your orders are all bark and no bite—all talk and no walk. You lose respect; people don't take you seriously. They're more critical of you and your actions—spreading negativity throughout your team.

Remember, the leader is a domino in a series of many dominoes. If you pull one domino out by saying one thing, then doing another, the whole chain is fouled up.

We All Want to Be Respected

In every relationship and every interaction, humans want respect. But so often in the workplace, bosses make their people feel like a package of new AAA batteries: they're glad to have the batteries, but don't really need them...until they need them. When your team members don't feel like they add value until you need to *use* them, they feel disrespected. They won't follow you—and they won't care to follow *through*.

One of the worst bosses I ever had was a guy we'll call Matt. When I reported to Matt, as was the case with most of my career, I was on the road a lot. And like every good manager should do, he required a regular one-on-one check-in call.

Matt would spend the first five or ten minutes telling me what was on his mind, making sure I knew how important he was, what big decisions he was making, and what I needed to do for him to actually execute on his commitments. Then, he would say, "Okay, Kyle, what's on your plate? What can I do for you?"

I'd start walking Matt through my list—and invariably, his attention drifted to something he must've considered more pressing, like his email! I could always hear him typing on the other end of the line: he was literally checking and sending emails during our meeting. Many times, I would check my email after one of our calls and there would be an email from him, sent *while we were on the phone*, about something unrelated to anything we'd been talking about. Or even worse, occasionally Matt would send an email asking me a question about something I had just explained during our call.

It was obvious he didn't care much about what I had to say. I'd finish a story or scenario, and more than once, he'd respond with a question about something I had literally already addressed. Or worse, I would finish a sentence, and there would be this long silence. You could almost hear his brain going, "Oh shit, Kyle's gone quiet. It must be my turn to talk."

"Sure," he'd say. "That's totally right."

What? Why the hell are we even having this meeting?

Well, it was on a checklist for him: "have one-on-one with Kyle every week." *Check.* Moving on. Matt's lack of respect for me and my time made me disrespect him as my boss—I certainly didn't see him as my *leader*. These interactions left me feeling *disen*gaged because *he* wasn't engaged.

As a result, I eventually stopped trying to contribute during these meetings. I listened to what he had to say and sometimes volunteered one or two things that were relevant, but everything else I just managed on my own.

Sidenote: you've probably gathered I'm not a fan of check-the-box one-on-ones. They can be incredibly valuable—but they should always be for the benefit of the team member, not the boss.

Leaders owe everyone on their team the same level of respect they require *from* the team. Period—no exceptions. You make this commitment when you become their leader, and it's your job to follow through by demonstrating your respect for their work, not to mention their time. You must be present, giving your full attention, looking out for their best interests, and providing them with guidance and support.

> You must be present, giving them your full attention, looking out for their best interests, and providing them with guidance and support.

If you *can't* do that...Well, there's no better way to tell someone, "I don't really give a damn about you."

Consider the people you lead: they want to lean on you and lean on each other. They want to follow someone they trust. They crave consistency and want to feel respected. In all those ways, they're exactly like you.

So how can you use your understanding of what motivates your people to inspire them to follow through? Let's start talking specific strategies.

Creating a Follow-Through Culture

Consider this scenario:

Let's say I've got a complex report due for my boss. I might need to request several of my team members to collect different information. I've got Sonia bringing me something, I've got Jeferson bringing me something, and I've got Eddie bringing me something. I'm going to be combining all those "somethings" into one cohesive report.

I've committed to get that report to my boss by Thursday, setting an expectation upon which I need to deliver. However, I can't deliver on my promise if my people aren't living up to their own commitments to me. It's tempting to blame a teammate for their failure to keep their commitment—but as we've discussed, it's on the leader to create a follow-through culture. If you want to consistently deliver on what you say you're going to do and set the example for your team to do the same, here are some strategies to help.

Be Painfully Clear about Expectations

Ambiguity is the enemy of execution. When it comes to efficiently delivering on commitments, ambiguity is bad news for everyone involved.

Ambiguity is the enemy of execution.

Consider this classic Corporate America scenario: We're in a team meeting and somebody brings up a good idea. I say, "Great!" Then I turn to Melinda, who's looking for a project. "Melinda, can you take that?"

Melinda nods and smiles, maybe even writes something down. "Got it, Kyle!"

And then we move to the next item on the agenda.

Whoa, whoa, *whoa*. What is the "that" she's taking? What is the "it"? Is there a due date? What about specific formatting? Is she to send me an email, a presentation, a smoke signal? Is it possible that neither Melinda nor I fully understand what we've just mutually committed to here?

I'm no psychic, but in this situation, I can absolutely foresee trouble ahead. Melinda will do her best to deliver but ultimately bring me something short of what I expected. And if I'm the classic corporate, outcomes-focused *boss* who is all about the "me" and not the "WE," I'm sure you can predict who will be blamed for this mess. Sorry, Melinda.

But in no way is this Melinda's fault. It's the leader's job to end every one of those meetings—hell, even some individual conversations—with a summary of *who* is on point to deliver, *what* they're expected to deliver, and *when* it should be delivered.

This might seem robotic or unnecessary. It's neither. The beauty of being this disciplined becomes obvious once Melinda and I repeat this cycle a few times. We'll eventually get to the point where she won't let an assignment pass without pushing to align on due date, formatting, and so on. If I fail to set those expectations, she'll be comfortable speaking up to do so.

No leader should foster or even allow such ambiguity, especially when their people are the ones who suffer the most from it—it's a waste of their time.

Make eye contact with the folks who are on point. Get visual confirmation from body language. Get vocal agreement. Do everything you can to make sure expectations are aligned. That's the first step toward *your* follow-through.

Then, either during the meeting or after it ends, calibrate on next steps. Be painfully explicit about details for the deliverable, making sure everyone involved agrees on these details. You've got to establish *what* is to be delivered, *when* it will be delivered, and *who* will do what—and the sooner we do this, the better the chances that the task is completed the right way from the jump.

> You've got to establish *what* is to be delivered, *when* it will be delivered, and *who* will do what. Make sure everyone involved agrees on these expectations.

Failure to align at the outset results in subsequent follow-ups to establish what should have been agreed upon initially. Or worse, iterating until you find exactly the right sweet spot. It's on the leader to be deliberately conspicuous about the expectations, and it's on the team member to ask questions if there is any ambiguity about any part of those expectations.

If something goes wrong along the way or something isn't delivered, it's easier to manage when everyone involved can lean against the expectation originally set. It's much harder to lean against unclear, or worse, unestablished expectations. It's like trying to catch smoke with your hands. That's why, in addition to clearly verbalizing your expectations, you and your team should also have systems to document decisions and/or deliverables.

Write It Down

It's a fact: documenting important tasks exponentially increases the likelihood that I'll actually do them. Writing it down and making it physical creates an Accountability Contract for me, with me. Getting it out of my head is key.

> Writing down expectations and making them physical creates an Accountability Contract.

I recommend you do the same—and lead your people to follow suit. Use some sort of note-taking medium during meetings and phone calls. It doesn't have to be anything fancy, and digital is likely best, if only because it's usually searchable and easily shared. If you're old school, good old-fashioned pen and paper still works. (I often use Post-its for this kind of thing and stick them to my monitor—a place I'm guaranteed to see them.) If I'm on the road, I use my phone to email myself. Then, when I'm back in the office, I'm guaranteed to have several emails requiring some type of action or response. The one I sent myself gets the same attention.

In a group setting, you should utilize meeting minutes and post-mortems, which have the benefit of being documents everyone can see. You can take this one step further by ensuring a follow-up email is sent to everyone who was in that meeting—again, including yourself—to establish accountability for everyone involved. In that email, identify *who* is supposed to do *what*, by *when*. This too, might sound like overkill. And at first, it might be. However, the time spent to memorialize takeaways and expectations from a meeting is but a fraction of time spent in rework and realignment. Eventually, this approach becomes standard protocol.

Of course, there are situations in which you may not be able to take notes or write it down yourself. If I'm in a casual hallway conversation with a team member, and he says, "Oh, by the way, Kyle, I need _____," then I'll often reply with, "Great. Send me an email on that, and I'll make sure I get on it." Once that email hits my inbox, we have a contract.

This still fits the bill of "writing it down," but now I've put the impetus for writing on the person who needs something from me. Just like the email I sent myself, this *to-do* is now in my queue.

Consistently Follow Up

Those notes might get lost. Those emails might get buried in your inbox. So let's go with a belt-and-suspenders approach: make sure you're following up, verbally or in writing, on promises made.

Earlier, I shared an abysmal check-in experience with my boss, Matt. However—when done the right way, check-ins can be a powerful leadership tool. You can do so via scheduled conversations or email, of course. Following up on a deliverable is less about making sure that my team member is working on it and more about making sure they know I'm here to help. Once we have agreement, I always trust the team member is working the issue. But my follow-up gives the team member even more opportunities to lean on me for guidance or help knocking down a barrier. Consistently following up on progress also sends the message that you consider this task a priority.

For keeping track of efforts of my direct reports, I use a note-taking app on my iPad. So, for example, if I have seven direct reports, I have seven "chapters" for them in the app, one for each direct report: Bradey, Curt, Karie, and so on.

When Karie and I meet, topics requiring follow-up are documented in the Karie chapter. I keep it incredibly simple, writing, "Karie owes me _____ ; I owe Karie _____ ," along with the agreed upon due date. Then, in subsequent meetings, I use the chapter as a rolling punch list, crossing off completed, overdue, and upcoming items as needed.

I look at those notes before every meeting with Karie. So when we talk, I'm able to reference them directly. For short-term deliverables, I might lead with, "Karie, we agreed last Monday that you would have X, Y, and Z prepared for this week. Can we start with X?"

For longer-term deliverables—say, something we talked about on September 20 that we agreed should be ready by October 15—I make sure to keep up with the progress at my September 27 meeting with Karie: "Hey, how's that mid-October deliverable coming? Is there anything I can do for you or any resources you need?"

This is my way of keeping an ongoing tally of obligations I've made to my team members and they've made to me. We're saying it again, and we're writing it down again—the best way to ensure that everyone follows through.

But I'm not naive—this kind of accountability can be difficult to maintain, especially with a big team. And managing my direct reports is one thing, but I also have to manage my boss and manage disparate operating groups who don't often communicate with one another. It's relatively easy to throw orders out, but it's pretty damn tough at times to follow up to make sure everything is getting done.

Make it as easy on yourself as you can. Use the tools that work best for you. Set reminders on your calendar; make that to-do list in various forms. Delegate point people for accountability as warranted.

No Matter What, Always Communicate the "Why"

I'm a firm believer that people are much more responsive, understanding, and professional when they understand *why* they've been asked to do something, even when they disagree with it. For most, the "why" enables people to care more and find greater satisfaction in their work—or if they're not more satisfied, they're certainly less grumpy.

In communicating the "why," I show you you're important and you matter enough to know. Of course, you are entitled to not like what I'm saying. You may even disagree with my position or with what I'm asking, but you'll always understand *why* I'm saying it and ultimately *why* I asked you for the help. And hopefully you'll feel respected knowing that I cared enough to share it with you.

And if you do disagree, we can talk about that—we *should* talk about that. In fact, it's your obligation to share your disagreement with me (along with the facts that support your position).

Communicating the "why" connects effort to outcome, plain and simple. It communicates respect to your people and bolsters their trust in you as a leader.

Publicize and Celebrate Follow-Through

The leader is obligated to share misses, create action plans, and even fire a team member when necessary. However, leaders have an equal or even greater obligation to celebrate a job well done. Acknowledging when someone knocks it out of the park is a critical element within a Culture of Excellence.

When a person is recognized for a job well done, they feel valued. They're afforded a genuine warm and fuzzy moment in which they feel proud of the accomplishment. And, just as important, others share in that pride. An enormous amount of goodwill is gained by conspicuously celebrating when someone has delivered and achieved success. The positive morale is paid forward, and momentum builds, inspiring others to do the same.

So, how do we celebrate? Not a silly question.

First, be mindful of different approaches for each member of the team. Think about your people, their likes and dislikes, and plan accordingly. Some people don't like the spotlight, so in that case, an "attaboy" delivered one-on-one goes a long way. Or even an email congratulating them on the achievement, with a cc to *your* leader, can be meaningful. If they're comfortable in a group setting, giving them a shout-out during a meeting or town hall is a tremendous compliment. If it's going to be a public venue, and the win warrants it, consider including your leader or even your leader's leader. Publicly sharing success "up" says a lot about your commitment to your team while shining the spotlight on a deserving team member.

> Publicly sharing success "up" says a lot about your commitment to your team while shining the spotlight on a deserving team member.

In any scenario, whether the situation warrants a verbal kudos, an email, a text, a news bulletin, a gift—whatever the right venue or medium is—recognizing and rewarding positive results comes with the leadership territory.

I can imagine some of you making a face right now: "But what if I'm not comfortable doing that kind of thing?"

Um, *get* comfortable with it.

I don't care how seasoned you are or how long you've been working: everyone loves and *needs* authentic praise. However, for reasons I'll never understand, some bosses act as if the more senior their position, the less they are obligated to celebrate with the team. That is total garbage leadership. The CEO of a Fortune 500 company can still blush when the board announces what a good job they've done. We're all seeking acknowledgment and the sense of pride that comes with recognition. So get on board. Work is hard, especially when so many positions are overburdened. Words of praise are free of charge, and they're another essential form of follow-through when you're a leader.

> Work is hard, especially when so many positions are overburdened. Words of praise are free of charge, and they're another essential form of follow-through when you're a leader.

Of course, there will be times when you need to balance praise with pay. If you've got someone on your team who's consistently delivering wins and garnering praise, eventually they will expect more than just a "Great job!" during a team meeting. Good work needs to be adequately compensated.

Nothing matters more than the people around you. Show them you value them *and* their contribution. Follow *through* on your commitments to them, follow *up* on their commitments to you, and celebrate the wins even as you improve from the misses.

What Are the Benefits of a Follow-Through Culture?

Following through on your commitments is a form of doing the right thing. And as you may have heard once or twice before, WE do the right thing. Always.

Establishing a reputation as someone who consistently does what they say they're going to do creates a brand for yourself that exudes authenticity and speaks to your trustworthiness.

And trust, in and of itself, is a benefit. Both your customers and your team expect you to deliver on your commitments to them. Your consistent follow-through converts their expectations into brand trust and loyalty. That trust becomes a foundational part of your relationship with both groups—on the macro level with clients and on the micro level with your teams.

Finally, clearly setting your expectations for what follow-through looks like provides everyone clarity of where the finish line is and how to get there. Having this alignment makes it a hell of a lot easier to reach the finish line.

Be a leader. Do what you say what you're going to do. Then demand the same from your team.

CHAPTER 4

WE
TAKE ACTION.
TAKING ACTION AND
MAKING A MISTAKE
IS OKAY.
BEING IDLE IS NOT.

" THE SECRET OF GETTING AHEAD IS GETTING STARTED. "

—MARK TWAIN

WE 4

At the end of that very first presentation on the 10 WEs in Lawrence, Kansas, there was an open dialogue for questions and discussion. One of the folks in the audience was Bob.

I've worked with guys like Bob for a long time. Bob was a senior member of the team who probably had around one thousand people reporting to him. At the time, I was still relatively new in my role, so I didn't know Bob well, but I would come to learn he's one hell of a good guy.

During the open dialogue, Bob said, "Kyle, this talk has really been great. So, can we start working through these 10 WEs with the leaders who report to us and their teams?"

I couldn't help but find it ironic that this guy—who's responsible for so many employees—felt he had to get permission to have culture conversations with his team. And he was asking in front of all his peers in that organization—dozens of other leaders just like him.

Half joking, I replied, "I don't know, Bob. *Can* you?"

After an awkward pause, he let out a big laugh. I laughed as well. We joked about that moment for years afterward.

But think about it: Who would stop him from investing time and energy on a topic this important with his employees? Who would stop him from driving a Culture of Excellence? Having those conversations with his team was entirely his call. He knew it, and I knew it—but he wasn't used to *doing* it.

His question highlights a lack of courage that is so widespread in Corporate America that even strong leaders, like Bob, can fall into. Bob was essentially asking if it was okay to take action to improve. In many companies, even senior leaders feel they need to get approval from their leaders before taking action—especially when it involves thinking outside the box and being creative.

If you feel like Bob—like you have to ask—it's a good thing you're reading this chapter.

WE 4, WE take action, is the follow-on to WE 3, WE say what WE're going to do. Taking action *is* the follow-through. Of course, we must weigh the risks, sure, but we still have to *do* the damn thing.

We often hesitate to take action because we're afraid to make a mistake. But mistakes are inevitable. And even failure is inevitable. In fact, both mistakes and failure are integral to success—at the very least, they're part of the learning process.

In Corporate America, we need to shift our thinking away from the fear of making a mistake. Fear of failure is not justification for avoiding taking action.

Take the pharmaceutical industry, for example, where there is a constant need for innovation and action. According to the *Journal of the American Medical Association*, the average research and development investment required to bring a new drug to market ranges from hundreds of millions to over $1 billion.[6]

Yet, in spite of the enormous expense, less than *14 percent* of all drugs in clinical trials eventually secure FDA approval.[7] Does this mean 86 percent of all new drugs are failures? No.

A "failed" new drug doesn't signify the end of the line for all the work put into it. Tamoxifen, which is now used as a hormone

---

6   O. J. Wouters, M. McKee, and J. Luyten, "Estimated Research and Development Investment Needed to Bring a New Medicine to Market, 2009–2018," JAMA 323, no. 9 (2020): 844–853, doi:10.1001/jama.2020.1166.

7   MIT Sloan Office of Media Relations, "Measuring the Risks and Rewards of Drug Development: New Research from MIT Shows That the Success Rates of Clinical Trials Are Higher than Previously Thought," MIT Sloan, January 31, 2018, https://mitsloan.mit.edu/press/measuring-risks-and-rewards-drug-development-new-research-mit-shows-success-rates-clinical-trials-are-higher-previously-thought.

therapy to treat and prevent some types of breast cancer, was originally designed as a contraceptive. The erectile dysfunction medication Viagra was originally created to treat angina.

Here's the point: the manufacturers of these medications saw an opportunity to take action by bringing a new drug to market. These two drugs are examples of that action resulting in "failure." However, because these companies didn't sit idle, waiting for the perfect outcome, they still found success. While the eventual outcomes were far from their original intentions, the results were incredibly important to the company's bottom line and, more importantly, to the public.

I'll cover more about the value of mistakes later in the chapter. But all this to say: taking action and making a mistake is okay. Being idle is not.

What Does Taking Action Look Like?

Taking action is simply recognizing an opportunity for improvement *and* making a move to address that opportunity. It's taking initiative. If you spot an opportunity to improve a product or service, or the experience of your client and/or crew, you *must* act.

A Culture of Excellence weighs ramifications and calculates risks, but always takes action. Sometimes the biggest hurdle to a big transformation is simply taking the first step—avoiding "analysis paralysis."

How can leaders thoughtfully take action?

- **Think like you're the founder of the company.** Is there a process you wouldn't be doing if you owned the company? If so, that's ripe for challenging and considering potential alternative approaches. If you're the owner and a particular process or procedure does not add value—you must take action to do away with those processes. Ask, "Why the hell are we doing it?" Likewise, if you or your team aren't doing something that could add tremendous value to the company, client, or your crew, you must ask, "Why don't we do that?" There may be perfectly acceptable reasons for why you don't—the key is recognizing the opportunity and weighing its potential. Granted, you're probably not the owner of the company and may have limited authority in what you can do. As needed, follow the appropriate chain of command to explore a change. But if you have the authority to make that change directly—take action.

- **Choose to be curious.** Don't settle for the status quo just because something has "always been done this way." Instead, ask questions. Get everyone to ask questions. Investigate your processes. Instead, ask, "Could we possibly be doing this any better?" Or ask, "Does this make sense at all?" The answer to "why" a particular process exists often shocks me. The response I often get is typically very opaque, without a concrete explanation. Your "curiosity alarms" should ring loudly when the person or team responsible for executing a process can't explain its value. Seek ways to improve, and don't be afraid of provocative ideas. Instead, lean in to them.

- **Inspire.** A leader is responsible for inspiring that lean-in, "anti-status quo" gene in the team. In other words, the phrase, "We've always done it this way" should be considered profane. A WE-oriented leader inspires and instills confidence for the crew to *think* and engage with the work at hand—taking action if a process or outcome is subpar.

- **Work smarter, not harder.** Yes, I'm aware of how cliché that sounds, but it's true. Taking action doesn't always mean putting in more time or elbow grease. In fact, sometimes the best action results in a new process that *saves* you time. That's the point of working smarter: streamline everything nonessential, leaving time to work on the big stuff. But even an effort that results in time saved requires taking action first.

Later in the chapter, I'll say much more about how leaders build an action-taking culture. But first, we need to ask, "Why isn't this standard operating procedure in the first place?"

Idle Hands, Busywork

Idleness is one of the most pervasive and insidious characteristics in Corporate America, especially in big companies. And it's idleness—not to be confused with laziness (which simply can't be allowed)—that is the enemy of progress.

> **Idleness is the enemy of progress.**

Makes a great bumper sticker—but it's a fact: idleness undermines efforts to build a Culture of Excellence. Why? Well, there are plenty of reasons.

Safety in the Status Quo

In most environments, being idle is just safe. And it's true, you can make a pretty good living keeping your head down and doing whatever your boss asks: day in, day out. Lather, rinse, repeat. But how ridiculously unfulfilling is this approach?

When employees are asked to do *less* than they are capable of doing, self-confidence deteriorates and boredom sets in. But self-confidence is a foundational requirement for taking action. A team member caught between a shrinking sense of contribution and boredom is the perfect recipe for a status quo sandwich.

> **A team member caught between a shrinking sense of contribution and boredom is the perfect recipe for a status quo sandwich.**

If your people see value in keeping their heads in the sand because deviating from the norm could possibly lead to some kind of retribution, they've got every reason to walk like a lemming. And in fact, in a lot of environments, that's exactly what they do.

"Leadership" Has the Answers

An even more ubiquitous driver of idleness is the notion that "Leadership" has all the answers. I've been in plenty of corporate environments in which people use the word *Leadership* like it's someone's name. They say things like, "We're waiting on Leadership to make a decision." Similarly, there's another unseen faction known as "Management," which also apparently has *all* the answers: "Slow down, before moving forward, we need to run this by Management." As if some magical master plan for execution of all big ideas within the company exists in another dimension. (Probably one with gallons of gourmet ice cream hidden away in a special freezer somewhere.)

Spoiler alert: there is no master plan being hoarded in some mythical ivory tower. (And unfortunately, no gourmet ice cream either.)

There is no master plan because you *are* "Leadership." You *are* "Management." It's you. And when you have what you think is a good idea, you need to share that idea.

Unfortunately, that's not the paradigm in most companies. People wait for someone else to approve it, someone else to do it, someone else to take initiative and get the ball rolling. It's just safer this way, right? Well—then who's going to make it happen? The self-confident, courageous leader, that's who.

The truth is, transformative ideas are all around us. From the new hire in the corner cubicle to the tenured leader in the corner office, there is no license required for the identification of improvement opportunities. Don't wait for some vague authority to take action for you.

> From the new hire in the corner cubicle to the tenured leader in the corner office, there is no license required for identifying improvement opportunities. Don't wait for some vague authority's approval to take action.

Not Enough Time

There's another cliché that stands in the way of taking action: you must take one step back to take two steps forward. It may be cliché, but it's also a reality. Some people will tell you taking a step back is corporate blasphemy. It shouldn't be—change may require you to press "pause" (or even regress) on other tasks if you want to drive improvement. If you've got a flat tire, you can't keep speeding down the highway—you have to pull the car over and get out the spare. Many people feel they're just too busy to take that step back to initiate needed change. As a result, we keep trying to force the car down the road on the flat tire.

Yes, there are legitimate reasons and times when you shouldn't rock the boat. The worst time to strategize about making changes is when you and your team are already overloaded or crunched for time, even if that's the time when the problems in the process might be most glaringly obvious.

However, too often, people get mired in their routines and don't ever pause to consider whether the work keeping them so busy is actually adding value. If you're not in the middle of a crisis—think about all those tasks making you so busy. Is it possible the lack of time is driven by some activity that adds little or even no value? Probably. Could you find ways to make your or your team's work life easier? Likely.

In Chapter 7, I'll discuss connecting action to outcomes. If there isn't a clear line between the two, you might be staring at an opportunity to take action.

Not Enough Solicitation of Ideas

In many companies, there's simply not enough solicitation of ideas for innovation from those closest to the "real work" of serving the customer. Far too often, changes come almost exclusively from the boss. (There's that ivory tower again.) A directive is handed down from on high: "We're making a change, and this is how we do it from now on. Any questions?"

It doesn't make much sense that someone far removed from a situation is the one giving direction to the group who do the "thing" more than anyone else. Wouldn't the group closest to the "thing" know more? A good leader has the courage to own what they don't know and seeks input from those who *do know* before making a change.

A good leader has the courage to own what they don't know and seeks input from those who *do know* before making a change.

In most companies, the people interacting with the customer, either in person or otherwise, generally have the best insight into continuous improvement opportunities. They know what makes their job difficult. They know what could make it easier, more efficient, and likely deliver a better outcome. In fact, they know a hell of a lot more in all those categories than the "Management" apparition.

Those who know the most should be encouraged to share ideas. However, they're typically not asked for their input in any meaningful way.

The result: employees hesitate to speak up if no one's showing an interest in their thoughts—yet another reason why many corporations end up with cultures of idleness rather than action. It's a vicious cycle.

Pundits might argue, "So what? Plenty of corporations are still raking in millions, if not billions, per year. Sure, not *everyone* is working their hardest every day, but there's clearly enough 'action' happening that all these companies are turning a profit. That's good enough, right?"

"Right?"

What's the Worst That Can Happen?

The consequences of not taking action are the same for companies and employees as they are for sharks: if you don't keep moving forward, you sink and die.

Stagnation

Failing to take action leads to *stagnation*—both personally for individuals and more broadly as a company. In fact, *stagnation* and *idleness* are both terms for "doing nothing." Neither of those words should be in anyone's marketing vocabulary. Imagine using either of those to describe yourself in a cover letter or an interview!

On the micro level, most people can only do the exact same task for so long before becoming so bored or burned out that their quality of work suffers. Every single day is exactly the same. It's like death by a thousand paper cuts.

In that kind of personal stagnation, you get the same result every time. And expecting anything else is, well, the definition of insanity. It's going to be the same old shit, day in and day out. Without innovation, it never gets better.

> Failing to take action leads to *stagnation*—both personally for individuals and more broadly as a company.

On the macro level, stagnation takes the form of what's known as the "Incumbent's Curse," a phenomenon where companies are so enamored with their success, they fail to take action and miss the next innovation or radically new opportunity.

When the company is chugging along, only loosely concerned with expanding or innovating, you should be damn sure there are companies like Amazon, whose mission seemingly *is* anti-stagnation, that will come along and gobble you up. Amazon is a case study of the purpose-driven disrupter. They're looking for a better way to do what you've done the same way for years and years, and they're looking at it very differently from established companies' perspectives. Companies like Amazon devour organizations that let themselves stagnate. They've done it to brick-and-mortar retailers, like Kmart and JCPenney, that existed for over a century. And more recently, Amazon set out on a quest to disrupt the mail-order pharmacy business—get your popcorn.

Consumers have more choices than ever, and they aren't standing in line to do business with a stagnant company prone to inaction. In fact, they'll take action of their own—seeking alternative sources to fulfill their needs.

Courage Lost

Most organizations are chock-full of creative and brilliant employees with great ideas to improve the team and/or company. They are burning to share their ideas until they realize the boss is completely disinterested. The message sent: do what you're told and subscribe to the way it's always been done—innovation flame extinguished.

When team members are expected to do their job the same way, every day, without an opportunity to take action to make it better, the most creative employees lose courage and shut down their contributions. The entire company's ability to innovate suffers.

What happens when a company creates a culture of stagnation and robs its employees of their courage to take action? Mediocrity abounds.

Deterioration

Remember the shark metaphor from earlier? Let's bring it back: a shark dies when it stops swimming. In the same way, inaction is a killer. It kills individuals (figuratively), and it kills companies (quite literally). Inaction leads to deterioration of purpose, fulfillment, creativity, and quality—all of which impact the consumer experience.

> Inaction leads to deterioration of purpose, fulfillment, creativity, and quality—all of which impact the consumer experience.

Yet history is riddled with examples of companies that appeared to almost embrace their idleness—leading some companies to ruin.

Take for instance, Blockbuster Video, a textbook example of idleness killing a huge company. In the 1980s, Blockbuster was the be-all and end-all of the at-home movie entertainment industry. Their model worked, people loved it, and Blockbuster saw no compelling reason to innovate.

Around 1994, Blockbuster hung on through the shift from VHS to DVD format but maintained an identical business model, which relied on people coming to their brick-and-mortar stores to rent movies. However, in the late nineties, an upstart company named Netflix came along with a DVD-by-mail business model. There were plenty of signs that Blockbuster should revisit their own business model. They didn't.

In 2000, Blockbuster had the chance to acquire Netflix...and scoffed at the proposition. They'd dominated the market for so long, they couldn't imagine some red-envelope startup could possibly be a threat.

As shifting technologies, including media streaming, became more prevalent, stores began to shutter. After turning up their nose at Netflix, it took Blockbuster nearly four years to begin offering a DVD-by-mail subscription—an obvious attempt to mirror Netflix's business model. But their attempt to "innovate" came too late.

By the time Blockbuster filed for bankruptcy in 2013, twenty-five thousand employees had lost their jobs.

Pardon the pun, but this movie has been played many times: nothing is too big to fail.

Blockbuster died a slow and painful death, and at the heart of its death was a failure to take action: the company didn't foster a culture of creativity, courage, and innovation among its employees. Should we believe, in a company of twenty-five thousand employees, no one had any transformation ideas to move the company forward? *Someone* could have steered Blockbuster toward evolving into what Netflix eventually became, but didn't.

Contrast Blockbuster with Netflix. Netflix recognized there was a way to disrupt the brick-and-mortar business model of DVD rentals—finding a better way to get DVDs into people's houses and avoid all the late fees customers already hated.

Netflix was also an early recognizer of the digital revolution in media consumption. They saw the writing on the wall—the music industry had already gone through a transition to digital downloads, and Netflix paid attention.

Today of course, Netflix is widely recognized as the company that pioneered digital video streaming and is now producing its own award-winning content.

You could look at the Blockbuster flameout as an example of a big company losing its way. I see it differently. Companies are made up of people—they aren't just a "hive mind." So it was a person, or people, who sat idle. I can't imagine someone didn't see the train coming as the company sat stalled out on the tracks.

Steve Jobs once said, "Innovation distinguishes between a leader and a follower." A follower keeps their head down and executes the tasks placed in front of them. An innovator examines, questions, and even challenges those tasks.

The innovator asks *why*. And to quote another Jobs campaign, the innovator "thinks differently."

On that note, let's talk about specific ways you can lead your culture toward taking action.

It Takes a Village

Once an opportunity has been identified, what does it look like to take action, in a practical sense? For starters, it looks a lot like what I talked about in Chapter 3—say what you're going to do, then you do it. In the context of taking action as a team, you need to have a lot of collaboration and communication. So let's talk about a few strategies to help you do the damn thing.

Be Overt

Taking action involves problem identification, stating your path, declaring your approach, and documenting the whole of it. It's important to make sure your actions are clear to those around you.

A strong leader maps out the vision—including action steps, ownership, and timing required for execution.

Don't build the plan in isolation. Solicit the help of your peers and your team in charting a path toward your team's vision—it keeps *them* engaged and keeps *you* open-minded.

Being overt about expectations enables your people to understand your intentions and the implications involved with taking a particular action. It also ensures you avoid the redundancy of two (or more) people unknowingly working on the same project. Finally, this sort of explicit communication invites other knowledgeable voices to weigh in on the best approach. Without crystal clear communication, taking action will fail.

Foster and Reward Innovation

Earlier, I talked about how self-confidence suffers in a stagnant environment. To avoid this mindset, you must provide ways to make it easier for the team to share innovative ideas. Make it worth their time and effort (and brainpower) to offer solutions.

How to make it easier, you ask? It's not enough to just say, "Send me your great ideas!" There has to be a tool or medium for the team to submit their ideas. I'm talking about a *real* mechanism, not just happy-talk.

During a recent consulting engagement with a real estate investment company, I was speaking to a group of leaders about the benefits of taking action. I'd gotten to the point where I was doing my evangelizing thing—preaching the importance of "innovation" and "taking action"—and I asked how ideas were solicited from their employees.

"Well, we have a suggestion box," someone offered.

That's legit old school, right there. And there's nothing wrong with a suggestion box per se. It's passive, but it's a safe way to solicit ideas—so long as people use it and leaders check it. That wasn't the case with this crew.

Most of the executives in the room had a look of utter confusion. "We have a suggestion box?" someone asked. "Where is it?"

After several minutes of head scratching and neck craning, it became clear most people didn't even know the suggestion box existed. Certainly no one in "Management" was checking the box. "Ye olde suggestion box" was—*and maybe still is*—sitting somewhere in a forgotten corner with a bunch of ideas in it that nobody's ever seen.

And regardless of the mechanism used, the forgotten suggestion box symbolizes the biggest threat to only "talking the talk" when it comes to taking action: if there's no follow-through, and all the proverbial box ever does is collect ideas on the inside and dust on the outside, it's worse than having no mechanism at all.

Real mechanisms for eliciting innovation, such as the company's intranet, are active and formalized—so long as someone is formally assigned to receive and pass along submissions. Consider adding innovation elements to each team's routine, such as dedicated discussion time in meetings and booking time to follow up on former discussions.

Consider offering incentives, too, paid or otherwise. I recently helped a company establish a program that offered a percentage of savings achieved to the employee who came forward with the biggest cost-avoidance strategy. They also offered a similar incentive for anyone who came up with the best new revenue-generating idea. You can bet those paid incentives helped get employees' creative juices flowing.

Another approach involves adding a "WE Take Action" element to each team member's performance review. This is a formalized way to solicit ideas and adds the expectation of taking action. If one of your team members was responsible for generating a game-changing idea, by all means, that should be discussed and celebrated in their evaluation. If a financial reward is appropriate, include that too. You want the best and brightest members of the crew to feel safe, even compelled, to offer suggestions for improvement.

Sidenote: a Culture of Excellence doesn't "punish" team members for not generating big ideas for change. Doing so only results in people submitting half-assed ideas because they have to. Your people shouldn't feel forced to innovate, but rather encouraged, to tee up actionable ideas.

By measuring and rewarding deliberate steps to take action, your team members are more invested in the team's success. Certainly, some bad ideas will surface, and that's okay. You've still gotten them to think about taking action. Regardless of the outcome, you're creating an empowering culture where team members are motivated to move the needle, take action, and avoid sitting idle.

You want your people to be the best they can be in their role. Establishing a measurable standard for putting forward ideas shows the team you're not going to spoon-feed them and tell them what actions to take. You're making sure they recognize the importance of their voice and the value they can offer.

When you embed this philosophy at all levels of the organization, you promote ownership of the issues that stand in the way of excellence.

Publicize Action—and Logical Inaction

We've already established there will be times when you can't take action, for one reason or another. The best way to deal with that is to be open and up-front about it. Publicize what you're going to do and not going to do, and explain the reasoning behind the decisions you've made.

At Maximus, we had eleven locations across the US. Every month, my senior leadership team would bounce to a different site to conduct focus groups—usually five or six a day, including all levels of employees.

Within a week, we'd send out a list, essentially saying, "Here's what we heard from you." Throughout the course of the next several weeks, we overtly communicated the ideas we were going to pursue as well as those we weren't. "Thanks to Jeferson Pinheiro's suggestion, we're going to _____." Or, "Someone also suggested _____, but we're not going to do that. And *here's why.*"

Give credit to the people bringing the best ideas. Don't call out the people whose ideas don't work, but be very clear that you heard the idea, considered it, but cannot implement it—and explain *why* in the plainest of terms. You can help bridge the Leadership Gap by being transparent about what you intend to do or not do. This type of transparency shows all employees you're listening to their ideas for taking action, thoughtfully considering them, and implementing improvements. Doing so keeps people motivated to voice innovative solutions and helps shape a culture in which the crew is always looking for opportunities to take action.

> When you are transparent about your intended course of action, you can help bridge the Leadership Gap between you and the people who so often put forth the best ideas: the frontline employees.

Yes, It Really *Is* Okay to Make Mistakes

The next chapter is about the importance of owning mistakes, but I want to address a point here, too, because mistakes are an important part of taking action. You can't take action if you're afraid to make mistakes—so let's confront the mistake monster head-on.

Expect Mistakes

You can't expect people to take action if they are concerned they'll lose credibility if their idea doesn't bear fruit. Be clear with your team that you really do *expect* mistakes—and mean it.

When you set the expectation that new ideas *should* be generated, you should be clear that you expect mistakes as well. Not every swing results in a home run. But what does result is learning and eventual improvement. This brings me to my second point.

Mistakes ≠ Failure

Given that mistakes are a necessary by-product of taking action, in *no way* do mistakes equal failure.

I'm serious about this.

I'm aware most people don't see it this way, and I know there are situations in which mistakes *can* lead to failure on a catastrophic level, both personally and professionally.

However, in a WE-oriented culture, mistakes are expected, understood, and at times, even celebrated. The entire history of the building blocks of modern society is one of constant trial and error. If the Wright brothers had given up after crashing their first prototype airplane, it's possible that powered flight wouldn't have existed for another several decades.

We learn, evolve, and become better from our mistakes because we identify what *not* to do—positioning us closer to the real solution. Consider the advances in artificial intelligence: much like humans, AI programs learn from mistakes and grow more sophisticated with every step. This leads me to my third point.

Mistakes = Building Blocks

If we recognize mistakes are not failures, then we must use them as building blocks or even data points. When you know a mistake was made because of X and Y reasons, you also know neither X nor Y is the answer. Many times, continuous improvement is simply guided by the process of elimination.

For instance, let's say I've identified three routes I can take to get from my office to my home. On Monday, I take one; Tuesday, I take the next; and Wednesday, I take the third. I'm going to rate each of those trips to find the quickest, most efficient route home, but does that mean the other two are mistakes? No, they're simply other possibilities that weren't optimal.

And that doesn't mean the lessons learned from the other two routes won't come in handy. I'm in downtown Tampa, next to an arena that is home to the Tampa Bay Lightning and several concerts. There's always the chance my usual route could be blocked off for the evening. However, thanks to my knowledge (building blocks) of the other two routes, when there is an event scheduled, I can rely on my alternative routes.

Learn as much as you possibly can, and let the information serve as a resource when unexpected roadblocks (pun intended) come up.

What's the Takeaway?

The key to WE 4 is simple: sitting idle will never advance the mission of your company, your client, or your crew. When you identify an opportunity to improve, take action.

If you want to have a lasting impact, you should have a reputation as one who takes action. For me, the greatest impact is sharing in a team member's satisfaction and fulfillment when the action they suggested drives positive change. Leading a team that is committed to taking action makes leading fun while simultaneously improving employee engagement and the customer experience.

Be responsible, though—nobody likes a cowboy in the workplace, so unless you are the "owner" of the domain involved, make sure you've properly vetted the idea before taking action. If you need additional capital or other resources, follow the appropriate chain of command.

To be clear, it doesn't take funding to promote this principle. And it doesn't take extra resources to inspire your team to fight the status quo.

When you and your team take action, there will be mistakes. Just own and use the mistakes as data points to help you improve. Easier said than done? That's why the next WE details the value of owning mistakes within a Culture of Excellence.

CHAPTER 5

WE

OWN OUR MISTAKES.
WE'RE NOT JUDGED
BY OUR MISTAKES.

WE'RE JUDGED BY HOW
QUICKLY **WE** REMEDY THEM.

AND IF **WE** REPEAT THEM.

"

ONLY THOSE WHO DARE TO FAIL GREATLY CAN EVER ACHIEVE GREATLY.

"

—ROBERT F. KENNEDY

WE 5

I f you have the courage to do the digging, gold can be mined from a mistake. Just ask the former CEO of Ford, Alan Mulally.

When the aerospace engineer and former Boeing executive was brought on as the CEO of Ford in 2006, Mulally was tasked with unifying Ford's divided global operations, transforming its lackluster product offering, and overcoming a dysfunctional culture. Mulally asked managers to color-code their status reports: green for "good," yellow for "caution," and red for "problems"—a common management technique to help quickly identify areas needing attention. Even though the company was facing a $17 billion loss, during his first few meetings, every leader coded their operations green, meaning "good."

Now, I haven't spent a single day behind the curtain at Ford. But I'm certain, in a company that size, with thousands of employees, it's patently impossible for every operation to be "good." Obviously, the managers at Ford were reticent to share underperforming and even failing operations with the new boss. To his credit, Mulally didn't buy the self-reported "health" of each of the operations. He urged the managers to think long and hard about their assessments, ask new questions, and come back with a more objective view.

At the same time, one of his executives was dealing with a major issue—a malfunctioning lift-gate actuator on the Ford Edge—that was so perplexing, he was forced to halt vehicle production. (Always an incredibly expensive move in manufacturing.) This brave leader brought a bright red readout to the next status meeting. Mulally outright applauded it, literally. A few weeks later, those all-green reports resembled something more like a Skittles ad. "At that moment, we all knew that we were going to trust each other," Mulally would later say.[8] "We were going to *help each other* to turn the reds to yellows to greens."

My favorite part of the story, though? That brave executive to first report a red status was Mark Fields, Mulally's eventual successor as CEO at Ford. (Score one for doing the right thing, leading by example, *and* owning mistakes.)

The $10 Million Mistake

Fields showed incredible courage and leaned in to his peers and new leader for help. His transparency and the lasting impact it had

---

8   David Muller, "Facing $17 Billion Loss, Color-Coding Helped Alan Mulally Turn Around Ford," MLive.com, July 24, 2016, https://www.mlive.com/auto/2016/07/alan_mulally_ralph_nader_induc.html.

on Mulally and the senior team at Ford reminds me of a story when one of my own team members, Nick, did his best to navigate his ownership of a $10 million mistake.

Although our professional lives have led us down different paths, I've been lucky to stay in touch with Nick. He was kind enough to provide his written take on the situation, so I'll share it with you here:

In the Spring of 2019, we were going through a repricing effort for our customer. I was charged with completing the call-volume forecast that would act as the basis for the repricing exercise. With hundreds of millions of dollars at stake, this was no small task.

I partnered with our data scientist, and we worked day and night for about a week to meet our deadline. When it was all said and done, we were going to be able to save our customer a lot of money—in the range of about $15 million that year. We presented the revised forecast and savings to our customer. As you'd expect, they were really pleased with the potential savings but asked for a few minor adjustments.

That evening, as we began working through adjustments, we realized we made a serious mistake. We double-counted a particular call type reduction and as a result...our original numbers were massively incorrect.

I immediately felt ill. I wondered: if I didn't say anything, would anyone really know? The truth is, no one would have discovered the mistake until we had significantly more calls than expected, poor service, and an even angrier customer. That's when the 10 WEs made the next step clear. I knew, "WE do the right thing—always" and "WE own our mistakes" no matter how difficult it may be. I called Kyle and let him know about the mistake. He was clearly disappointed in the situation but thanked me for being honest and letting him know. He had the unenviable task of going back to our customer and informing them the savings were going to be about $10 million less than we anticipated, due to this error.

I couldn't sleep the entire night. I kept questioning myself: "Do I really belong here? Do I have what it takes to contribute to this team?" My self-confidence was gone. The next day I asked Kyle if he had a minute to talk. I apologized again and let him know I was struggling with my mistake.

Kyle let me know that he knew I was the right person for the job. He said if he ever questioned my abilities or his trust in me, I wouldn't have been in that position in the first place. He picked me up (WE pick each other up) when I really needed it, despite the problems my mistake created for him. He didn't judge me based on my error. He was appreciative of my honesty and the initiative I took to fix the problem.

I hugely respect Nick for the courage it took him to own that mistake and appreciate him for allowing me to use his words. His response is a textbook example of what to do when you screw up: assess it, own it, and try like hell to fix it—and you communicate all of this to the people on your team so they can help.

The crux of the matter is this: We are human. Humans screw up. It's a given. You can allow screwups to crush you, or you can own them and recognize the mistake for what it is—a growth opportunity. WE 5 reinforces the idea that making mistakes is a necessary part of taking action. And just as important, use the mistake to prevent errors from happening in the future.

> You can allow screwups to crush you, or you can own them and recognize the mistake for what it is—a growth opportunity.

Mistakes Are Both Inevitable and Good

Before we get into the importance of mistakes, I need to insert a disclaimer:

Not all mistakes are created equal, and some mistakes are more forgivable than others.

A mistake made from *carelessness* can be tolerated and forgiven—once. However, carelessness can be pervasive, and accepting the same mistake more than once sends all kinds of bad messages to your crew.

A mistake made from *malice*, however, can't be tolerated at all. If someone lies, hides information, and/or knowingly fails to live up to their responsibilities, those mistakes all fall into this category and should be met with swift and decisive action. You simply cannot allow this behavior on your team.

There's a third kind of mistake, which is actually worth embracing: the good-faith mistake. I like to think *most* mistakes fall into this category: they're made in good faith while actively pursuing improvement. These are the kinds of mistakes that are the most important ones—the ones that can be gifts.

The good-faith mistake comes along when you're stretching yourself, when you're trying something new, and when you're doing something in a different way. As I covered in the last chapter, these mistakes are the ones that go hand in hand with "WE take action," and they're both inevitable and good. They can and should result in positive change, both on a micro and a macro level.

Throughout my career, I've seen how a good-faith mistake can lead a team to a better place. Nick's story is a good one in this regard: once he identified the mistake, he and his team worked to create a more rigorous review process, improving accuracy.

In another instance, years ago while working at a health plan, our IT team was making changes to the call center routing schema, which required taking the system down, making the changes, then putting it back up. Well, they skipped a step in the process. When the system went back up, multiple callers went to a busy signal and couldn't reach anyone at the call center—that's a disaster.

Luckily, the person in IT responsible for the mistake realized what happened and owned it. She started the chain of communication, which led to me getting a call from the VP on my team. Because of this, we were able to quickly react, and we reached out to customers directly to limit the negative effects.

We owned the mistake our callers were forced to endure. However, the real silver lining of this incident was that, because the team member in IT took ownership of her mistake, IT was able to develop a new checklist when performing this kind of update to make sure it would never happen again. This woman's mistake and her willingness to own it, ended up benefiting countless people in the long run because that step in the process could have otherwise been skipped again in the future. Who knows how long it might have taken the team to figure it out if no one had come forward? The fact that this woman did was a gift that helped the customer, the company, and our call center team.

Think of an accounting mistake: if you don't own it, either it will resurface next month, when you correctly close the books. Or, if you perpetuate the same calculation error, it will only snowball and grow every month. There's no "covering it up," and it's not going to magically fix itself—so isn't it better to get out in front and own it as soon as you recognize the problem? Owning mistakes early stops little mistakes from turning into big problems.

And Yet, Most Are Afraid to Own Mistakes

Owning mistakes is rarely even talked about in Corporate America. The blame for that lands on *bosses* at every level. This plagues most company cultures for two reasons: bosses are afraid of looking inept in front of their employees and exposing their vulnerabilities. And they're afraid of looking bad in front of their own *bosses* and jeopardizing their reputation. Of course, the team sees when the boss attempts to gloss over or downplay a mistake, sending the message, "Only admit fault when absolutely necessary."

So, what do members of the team do when they err? You got it: "Only admit fault when absolutely necessary." This cycle will indefinitely repeat until an authentic leader steps in.

When building a Culture of Excellence, you must shift the focus from *me* to *WE*, turning the analysis of the mistake from *who* to *what*. Don't spend energy focusing on the person, but rather, focus on the problem. Suddenly, you'll find it a lot easier to craft a culture where owning our mistakes is commonplace. But before we get there, let's shine a light on the fears holding most back from doing so.

Courage—Yes, Again

In the last chapter, I talked about the role courage plays in our motivation and ability to take action. The same is true for owning mistakes. A lack of self-confidence can take plenty of forms, and it exists at all levels within a firm. It's especially common in junior or inexperienced bosses, but it's even more tragic when you see it in tenured managers.

You see, many leaders function with a certain amount of imposter syndrome. They feel like making a mistake devalues them, hurts their credibility, and exposes them as someone who can't lead others. As a result, some leaders push the message they can do no wrong. If something does go wrong, it's probably someone else's fault. (Maybe yours!)

This type of boss tends to conflate "authority" and "accuracy," implying, "I'm the boss. I'm *right*. What I say goes. And don't question it." Then they double down on a mistake instead of owning it and working to fix the problem. News flash: this is not a great strategy for building a Culture of Excellence.

Here's why: let's say I'm leading my team on a hike. Two miles into the hike, I come to a fork in the path and decide to turn left. Within a quarter of a mile, pretty much everyone on the hike realizes we've made a wrong turn—including me, probably. But instead of turning around, I dig in and say, "I'm pretty sure this is right. Let's keep going."

Then I take another turn to the left, hoping to course-correct without having to admit my mistake. Two miles later, we're in a *really* bad place. Everyone knows we're lost, but I refuse to admit I led us in the wrong direction.

What happens in this scenario? My team starts shrinking. The best and brightest will be the first to realize their leader doesn't know what the hell he's doing. They'll split from the pack early, but it won't be long before most others get tired of being led down the wrong path as well. It's only a matter of time before they quit following me too.

And why shouldn't they? I'm wasting everyone's time and energy, including my own. There's every chance that one of them could actually direct the whole group of us back to the right path, but I'm not giving anyone the opportunity to help.

Conclusion: the hike is an epic fail. More specifically, my leadership on the hike is an epic fail.

This is a common scenario when working with an insecure boss. The more they stand their ground and refuse to own a mistake, the more the team suffers. In addition to the team mirroring the unhealthy behavior, other potential consequences include turnover, a lack of respect, a lack of trust, and a general sense of skepticism in the boss. Of course, as an authentic leader, there are times you must stand your ground, but if the entire team is telling you, "We need to turn around," you damn well better listen.

> As an authentic leader, there are times you must stand your ground, but if the entire team is telling you, "We need to turn around," you damn well better listen.

Stubbornness is one way insecurity rears its ugly head, but it also shows up in the form of timidity—and being a timid leader doesn't get the team very far either. Go back to the hike scenario: if I'm a timid leader, I might be so afraid of making a mistake that I sit down at the trailhead and don't bother leading us onto the actual trail. No one wants to be led by this person—cue the corporate mutiny.

If this sounds like you, not to worry. Take some encouragement from Tom Bilyeu, one of the founders of Quest Nutrition, who, by his own admission, initially fit the profile of a timid and insecure leader. Bilyeu's company started from zero before eventually selling for more than $1 billion.

Bilyeu pocketed a king's ransom from the sale, and he's dedicated the rest of his existence to helping people realize their full potential. (In Tom's podcast, *Impact Theory*, he closes every episode with two simple words: "Be legendary." I highly recommend it.) However, he's talked very candidly about how, in the beginning, he started out as a shy introvert who felt like he didn't know what he was doing. He was so scared of making a mistake or looking bad in front the team, he sat quietly through meetings and conference calls, sitting on the edge of his seat in anticipation for the end of the call. Tom saw the end of calls as his only window to confidently chime in without fear of screwing up. His contribution: "Take care, everyone—thanks!" *That* was his entire contribution.

Seeing him now, this story blows my mind, thinking about a guy trying to lead but dealing with so much fear while building his own company. However, Bilyeu was wise enough to see this approach would do nothing to help him reach his goals. He worked his ass off to eventually overcome his timidity and lead with more confidence. Now he inspires millions of people every day.

Good leadership doesn't mean being an immovable object. It also doesn't mean you hide under your desk. Good leadership requires you to listen to your people and change your position when it's necessary.

> Good leadership doesn't mean being an immovable object. It also doesn't mean you hide under your desk. Good leadership requires you to listen to your people and change your position when it's necessary.

Maybe you're thinking, "Wait—won't I have less authority or credibility if I change my mind on something? Nobody will follow a flip-flopper!" Not true.

Consider this quote from Apple CEO Tim Cook. When asked about leadership lessons he picked up from Steve Jobs, Cook answered, "[Jobs] would flip on something so fast that you would forget that he was the one taking the 180-degree polar [opposite] position the day before. I saw it daily. This is a gift, because things do change, and it takes courage to change. It takes courage to say, 'I was wrong.' I think he had that."[9]

Under Pressure

Looking bad in front of your people is one thing—but looking bad in front of your boss is a whole other ball game. In many companies, a mistake can leave you branded as unable to ascend to the next level. Or worse, the mistake leads to termination. This creates an unfair and unrealistic expectation, even if only self-imposed, implying you must be perfect or have very little room for error. Your take-home message: don't screw up. Or at least don't let anyone know you've screwed up.

With the pressure and potential fallout from a misstep, it's natural to weigh the option of not owning it. This is especially true when you are the one closest to the mistake. You might even go as far as calculating the odds of someone discovering your blunder. This was the option that Nick faced in the story I shared earlier. Hiding the mistake would have been the easy route, and it's possible that no one would have ever found out. If hiding a mistake means your reputation and your brand are preserved—couldn't that be a good thing?

Hopefully you come to the same conclusion Nick did: WE do the right thing, and WE own our mistakes. Nick chose the more

---

9   Peter Kafka, "Steve Jobs Was an Awesome Flip-Flopper, Says Tim Cook (Video)," AllThingsD, May 29, 2012, https://allthingsd.com/20120529/steve-jobs-was-an-awesome-flip-flopper-says-tim-cook/.

difficult path. But his path demonstrates far more integrity. When he chose to live up to these two WEs, in spite of what it could cost him, he earned my lifelong respect and admiration.

However, I can't help but wonder if that would have been the case elsewhere.

I get it; most cultures have a very low tolerance for *any* type of mistake. Fear of making a mistake—and the wrath that might result—is understandable. But this is yet another reason why you must lead by example in allowing for and requiring ownership of mistakes. Most bosses fail to realize the ultimate benefits that come with owning a mistake: when you own it, you help steer your company's culture in a healthier direction. You can look squarely in the Mirror of Truth. Owning it enables you to recruit support from the team. You also avoid the distraction that comes from worrying about the other shoe dropping when someone eventually finds the error. Instead of functioning as an island, you're leaning in to the collective power of WE.

Truth or Consequences

Bosses feel as though they must convey a sense of perfection—as if the title they've achieved somehow magically removes any potential for error. They'd prefer to stand proudly on a "Perfection Pedestal." But this pedestal mentality only widens the Leadership Gap.

One of my biggest goals of *Begin With WE* is to help create cultures where *nobody* within the company is on a pedestal—instead, everyone stands together, shoulder to shoulder. When everyone's on the ground, there's not nearly as far to fall...and in a WE-oriented culture, odds are, someone will catch you. After all, WE pick each other up. (Exactly why WE 6, "WE Pick Each Other Up" immediately follows this chapter.)

> **Create a culture where *nobody* within the company is on a pedestal—instead, everyone stands together, shoulder to shoulder. When everyone's on the ground, there's not nearly as far to fall.**

Here's the good news for leaders struggling with insecurity or fear—a fact that most bosses aren't vulnerable enough to learn—there's power in admitting you're not perfect. Owning a mistake for all to see makes you more relatable and trustworthy, especially to your crew. In fact, a 2016 Dale Carnegie Global Leadership study involving thirty-one hundred workers—from junior employees to CEOs—in thirteen countries, revealed **84 percent** of respondents want leaders who have the humility to admit when they are wrong.[10] (My first reaction: What the hell is wrong with the remaining 16 percent?)

---

10   Dale Carnegie Training, "Dale Carnegie Training Global Leadership Study USA—2016," United States Documents, January 3, 2017, https://documents.pub/document/dale-carnegie-training-global-leadership-study-usa-2016.html.

Joe Hart, CEO of Dale Carnegie, put it this way: "Employees are more satisfied with their job and more likely to stay when their leaders are honest, trustworthy and true to their beliefs."[11]

A dishonest and/or untrustworthy boss is the main culprit of employee dissatisfaction, leading to higher turnover. The study also showed that employees are more likely to be on the job hunt if their supervisor doesn't *admit to mistakes,* listen to employees, show appreciation for employees, or demonstrably value employee contributions.

Not convinced? Maybe you're thinking, "It's not like covering up my mistakes would have major consequences anyway."

Or would it?

As I covered in Chapter 2, leaders are always being observed, so everything we do has a ripple effect. This is undeniable when it comes to the consequences of failing to own mistakes. The impact is seen on three levels: macro, micro, and personal.

Macro

On the company level, if we don't own our mistakes, we're faced with a lack of growth—employees won't feel safe enough to take

---

11   Dale Carnegie Training, "Dale Carnegie Study Reveals the Connection between Leadership Skills and Job Satisfaction," June 29, 2018, PR Newswire, https://www.prnewswire.com/news-releases/dale-carnegie-study-reveals-the-connection-between-leadership-skills-and-job-satisfaction-300364541.html.

action and innovate for fear of making a mistake. Just as is the case with failing to take action, failing to own mistakes contributes to stagnation.

Also, trust and credibility become an issue for everyone: leaders, team members, and customers alike. Your company's brand reputation suffers when you don't own mistakes. This is especially true in the case of a blunder that's visible to the public. Bad news travels fast, and the slightest misstep can sink a company's image.

Micro

Not owning mistakes is particularly toxic within your team, because what develops too often is what I might eloquently refer to as "a culture of hiding shit." Mistakes happen—we've already acknowledged that—but if no one's talking about them, they're probably happening more often than you know. If we agree that socializing mistakes results in a safe space to share them, the inverse must also be true: the absence of the same dialogue promotes hiding shit.

Hiding shit is a slippery slope for members of your team. If one person is hiding their mistakes, you should assume others are too—or if they're not yet, they will. I always tell people that I can't help you fix a problem that I didn't know existed. Shining a light on a mistake is often the only way to get and give the support needed to make it right. This was never more evident than what I described with Alan Mulally and Ford.

Shining a light on a mistake is often the only way to get and give the support needed to make it right.

Here's the point: a culture that doesn't own its mistakes produces a team that covers shit up, struggles with disengagement, and deals with high turnover.

Personal

Then there's the Mirror of Truth: What will it tell you if you conceal a mistake? Why struggle with the concept of owning a mistake? Hiding the mistake only creates stress above and beyond what was caused by the mistake itself. Now you're spending time and energy on something that will probably come back to bite you in the ass at some point anyway. It can be liberating to just own it—let the truth set you free.

During "The $10 Million Mistake," Nick owned his error—but he wasn't the only one. As the leader of the team, I was ultimately responsible for the mistake, and I had to own it in front of the customer. I suppose I could have tried to bury it, but what example would I be setting if I did—not just for Nick, but his entire team and his peers? And worse, if and when the client found out, they would have been far more upset than if we'd just owned the mistake from the beginning. Besides, if I had deliberately tried to cover it up, you can bet I would have avoided eye contact with the Mirror of Truth.

The chapter is in part titled: "WE're Not Judged by Our Mistakes but by How Quickly WE Remedy Them." I'm a firm believer that most rational humans accept this notion. In my experience as a consumer, when something goes off the rails but the company owns it and goes above and beyond to make it right, I am endeared to that brand more than before the mistake even happened. They screwed up—they made it right—and that shows me they have integrity.

Consider this: your employees know you. Your direct reports, especially, know your strengths and weaknesses, just as you do theirs. When you own your shortcomings, you're simply confirming what they probably already know, and you're showing you're trustworthy to boot. Remember, as a leader, your behavior sets the example for your people to follow. You've got to practice what you're preaching, always, for the sake of your customer, your company, your crew—and in this case, yes, for yourself.

So, how do you do that? Let's get practical about what it looks like to effectively own your mistakes. I'll detail strategies and ways you can evangelize a culture of owning mistakes. And finally, I'll describe an approach to solutions that not only ensures your crew solves mistakes, but also guarantees no repeat offenses.

Leadership and Ownership

I can't stress enough: it's the leader's obligation to establish a workplace culture where team members are comfortable owning their mistakes. You've got to set the example by instilling trust and confidence that making a mistake will be met with support, not a pink slip.

Set the Example

Let's swing back to WE 2 for a moment: WE lead by example. One incident during my time at a company that will remain nameless sticks out to me. In a colossal mix-up, several boxes full of confidential patient data were mistakenly sent to another patient's home. Let me say that again—someone in my organization sent sensitive medical records of *thousands* of patients to one unsuspecting person's home. I may not have been the one to send out those boxes, but the incident happened on my watch. Ultimately then, this was my mistake to own.

I reported to the President of the company. And when this situation came to light, I knew I had to take my own medicine, call him to explain the situation, and accept responsibility for what I knew could very well be a fireable gaffe. I had come to know the President as a fair and pragmatic gentleman, but this was the first time I was faced with the uneasy scenario of owning not just a mistake, but a potential CNN-worthy fuck-up. Still, I knew it was the right thing, so I picked up the phone.

"Hey, boss," I said sheepishly. "I don't have all the details yet, but it appears one of the mail rooms in my org sent thousands of patient records to the home of one of our other patients."

I'll never forget his reaction. First, there was a pause. Then he said, "Well..." Long pause. "That's not good." He paused again. "That's bad, right?"

"Yeah, that's bad...very bad," I said, not sure if he was joking. (He was.)

"Okay. What are we going to do about it?" And just like that, he immediately shifted into problem-solving mode. We'd owned the mistake and quickly transitioned to fixing it and making sure it never happened again.

This conversation left me even more comfortable bringing mistakes forward in the future. In your own leadership, let this type of level-headed problem-solving response be your goal when an employee confesses to a mistake. When you set this kind of example, your people are much more comfortable being transparent with their own fumbles.

By calling him, I minimized the negative impact at the macro, micro, and especially personal levels. Imagine the example I would have set if, upon learning the news from the VP on my team who oversaw this area, I *didn't* call my leader? What message would I have sent, and how might she handle the next crisis? If I showed myself to be a hypocrite leader preaching about owning mistakes but not actually *doing* it, odds are she wouldn't even call next time. And who could blame her? If her *boss* hides mistakes— so can she.

As bad as this mistake was, it was also a gift. Clearly the mail room that shipped the boxes lacked the quality control needed to avoid this type of scenario. The VP who owned the mistake implemented a more rigorous checklist for outgoing packages—the very same day of discovery.

Get in Front of a Mistake and Provide a Solution

A company only exists because of its customers. Naturally, any mistake that impacts the customer must be dealt with—quickly, yet thoughtfully.

When the client is affected by a mistake, taking immediate ownership goes a long way in lessening the impact. Quick and transparent communication shows the client your commitment to doing the right thing. However, owning the mistake is only the first obligation; you must also come to them with the solution, or variety of solutions, to solve the problem. Don't wait for the perfectly executed postmortem, including every detail, before sharing the bad news. If the issue is rooted in something very complex, simply communicate the situation and commit to a detailed explanation as soon as practical.

> Don't wait for the perfectly executed postmortem, including every detail, before sharing the bad news. If the issue is rooted in something very complex, simply communicate the situation and commit to a detailed explanation as soon as practical.

With that said, there may be certain details worth leaving out. In the case of "The $10 Million Mistake," the head of the client's organization knew Nick on a first-name basis. In my phone call to her, I never used Nick's name, sharing only that "we" botched it. As far as the client was concerned, *we* screwed up, and the ultimate accountability sat with me.

When I own mistakes for my team (or myself) to a client, I pull no punches. I'm painfully candid, as if to take away any "ammunition" the client might use against me. If you just lay it out there and say how badly you screwed up, what's the worst they can say to you? Probably nothing you haven't already said to the Mirror of Truth. They might make you feel guilty or, worse, take their business elsewhere. But in most cases, they're mainly going to be concerned about your plan to solve the problem and avoid repeats. I've found owning the mistake actually results in greater trust from your client. The transparency you display when owning a mistake shows you're going to be straight with them, always.

It's almost always the leader's responsibility to have these tough conversations with the client. And candor narrows the gap between the client and the team: the team knows you have their back, and the client knows you have their best interests in mind.

So do the right thing and lead by example. Tell the client the ugly truth. Communicate it clearly with unflinching candor: "This mistake happened. Here's why and how it happened. Here's how and when we're going to fix it, and this is what we are doing to ensure it never happens again."

Explicit Communication

When someone is brave enough to come forward, it's important to ask questions—a lot of questions. However, the questions need to be crafted in a way so as to interrogate the *mistake*, not the person who slipped up.

Mistakes should ultimately be used as filters or checks within your quality assurance efforts. When a mistake occurs, examine each step in the process. Search for ambiguous or potentially unclear elements as well as steps with a high degree of difficulty. Pay special attention to processes that include handoffs, especially handoffs from one person to another (vs. one team to another). People-dependent processes can be a nightmare without disciplined checks and balances.

Here's a very basic example. Let's say step three of a process is, "Move the box from Table A to Table B." However, the first time I set the box on the end of Table B, the table collapses. Mistake! In order to complete step three correctly and consistently, I need to put the box in the *middle* of Table B. When I'm the only one doing this task, I've learned an important lesson and will most certainly avoid making the same mistake in the future.

However, someone new to this task may not realize the instability of the table. In the absence of those three words, "in the middle," the wide-eyed new employee might follow the written process to the letter—and now we're down two broken tables.

But if I record that "in the middle" variable as part of the process, I improve the efficiency of that step. Step three now becomes, "Put this item *in the middle* of this specific table." This required element also gets put into a checklist, and it becomes a mistake that your team will no longer make.

I've intentionally oversimplified this example for effect. However, the underlying message is important: don't assume *anything* when documenting processes. And much more importantly, don't assume the employee "failed" without first interrogating the mistake.

When the problem is more complex, take your interrogation deeper using a proven process improvement technique, the Five Whys.

The Five Whys

The Five Whys is a tried-and-true method for interrogating a problem or mistake. First used in the 1930s by the founder of Toyota Industries, Sakichi Toyoda, the process is still core to the company's quality assurance practices. My approach for this technique actually involves seven steps, but you still ask "why" five times.

Once someone has been brave enough to own a mistake, here's what you can do.

1. Assemble a team to gather the specifics of the problem. Consider including someone who knows very little about the process but is secure enough to ask what might be considered "stupid" questions. When someone has some distance from the situation, they're less likely to miss the forest for the trees, allowing for questions that people closer to the process may not think to ask.

2. Formally and succinctly define the problem at hand. Any medium works—I'm a whiteboard guy, so I love writing it out or drawing something to illustrate the problem.

3. Ask the all-important question: "*Why* did this happen?" Begin where you think is logical, then work backward from there if necessary. Asking "*why*" five times is usually enough to get you to the root cause of the problem. (Example: "The wrong item was pulled from inventory." "*Why*?" "The item we pulled was mislabeled." "*Why*?" "Our employee who labeled the inventory placed the wrong label on the item we pulled." "*Why*?") Keep going as needed. Your team will be able to intuit where to stop the questioning process.

4. Distinguish the root cause from symptoms in the answers you find. A symptom is a sign or indication of the root cause, not the cause itself. Symptoms usually aren't crystal clear and can be tough to categorize.

5. Assuming no malice was involved, address the *cause*—not the person or the team involved.

6. Agree on countermeasures (actions taken to prevent the problem from arising again).

7. Monitor those countermeasures. This step is often omitted but is just as critical as the previous six. Monitoring the countermeasures is the only way to know if the root cause has effectively been addressed.

I can't stress enough the importance of properly approaching the fifth step here. We are tough on problems and process, not on people. Like the example of placing the box on the table, too often the flaws originate from a faulty process or poor instructions; if those elements aren't precise, the blame cannot be laid solely or even primarily on the person.

While we can't fix human nature and our propensity to make mistakes, we *can* fix our processes and procedures.

Be an Expedition Leader, Not a Tour Guide

Exploring new approaches, processes, and procedures can actually be extremely fulfilling. Doing the same thing, day in and day out, is not.

Let's go back to the illustration of a leader setting out on a hike with their team. Imagine you've signed up to do a tour of a national park. You show up, pay your money, and set out with your tour guide. The tour guide tells you exactly where to go and insists you stay on the well-traveled path. He tells you what to look at, what to do, and drones on about facts in a way that makes it clear he's done this a million times before. When you try to venture onto a side path, he barks at you to stay on the main route, where it's safest. This tour might be interesting the first time, but you wouldn't want to take the same tour the next day. You certainly wouldn't want to repeat the same tour day in and day out.

But let's say you show up to this national park, and your guide treats it more like an expedition. She encourages exploration; she takes questions and feeds your desire for greater knowledge. She allows for some wandering off the beaten path, so long as you take proper precautions. The group starts to bond over the shared experiences, and you all begin to trade discoveries.

You end up making new friends and some cool discoveries. It's the kind of expedition you would do not once, not twice, but over and over. *That's* the kind of leadership needed to inspire an engaging, fulfilling, and risk-tolerant team environment. A *boss* is like a tour guide, leading the same hike every day, Monday through Friday, month in and month out. As a tour guide, you're the only one giving information, and you call all the shots; you're not inviting anyone else to contribute in any meaningful way. Where's the excitement when everyone on the tour knows exactly how it ends every time? There's no chance of making mistakes because there's nothing new, but there's also no adventure or collaboration. Boring.

On the other hand, if your team is challenged to try new things and the trek is a journey filled with collaboration, you're an expedition leader. When you're more than a tour guide, the team has an idea of the destination—we all know, on some level, where we want to end up—but no one individual knows exactly how we'll get there. You *are* the person responsible for blazing the trail and leading the crew on an expedition full of perils, pitfalls, and challenges.

As the leader of an expedition, you must go deeper. You must be brave. You must be comfortable with ambiguity. In serious expeditions, the extent of your knowledge of the road ahead might be limited to only the very next step in front of you—and then the next step, and so on. So naturally, you've got to be ready for mistakes and course corrections. You need to own them, constantly seeking input from your team along the way, using their input to help inform your decisions. In a Culture of Excellence, when members of the crew recognize you're going down the wrong path, they are confident enough to speak up, and the leader is open and ready to make the necessary adjustments. There is a sense of equity and collaboration that will enrich the entire journey.

I love this analogy because we've all been there—the proverbial tourist, fanny pack and all—whether being led by a guide in a museum, a national park, or even white water rafting. My favorite is the guide who drones on and on through a barely decipherable PA system while guests politely nod and smile (having no idea what was just said).

The leader doesn't always have the path perfectly charted but has faith in their ability and recognizes the value of others' input. The leader has the ability to make the experience fabulous—or monotonous.

Owning Mistakes Benefits Everyone

I remember a tiny screwup of my own that still looms very large in my brain. Years ago, I was asked to do a 10 WEs refresher for an expanded audience of leaders. I was rolling through the presentation, as I'd done countless times, when I clicked on a new slide and looked at the screen.

There was a typo in the text.

In the "WE Obsess Over Details" section.

I saw it and froze. I made a few slide edits that morning and just blew it. Given what I was preaching, I was mortified.

Facepalm.

All I could do was own my mistake. "Shit! Well, I blew it, guys. I'm so sorry," I said. "No excuses, I didn't give my presentation the attention I should have."

But what happened next inspires me to this day. The group roasted me—deservedly so. We had a good laugh together, then got right back to business—no tension, no weirdness. Yep, I blew it, but the crew's reaction confirmed we were in an environment where making a mistake was accepted and embraced—even with humor.

WE 5 enables an environment more focused on problem resolution than finger-pointing. When WE own our mistakes, everyone benefits:

- The **client** benefits because the product and/or service continually improves as you address and learn from mistakes. Clients have fewer complaints in the long run because they recognize your transparency and dedication to continuous improvement.

- The **crew** and **company** benefit because you're creating an open and inviting culture—one where team members are encouraged and expected to own and share their mistakes without fear of blowback. It's a powerful thing to work within a team that isn't terrified of screwing up or getting fired because of a good-faith mistake. The result is improved employee engagement as well as higher employee and customer retention.

- You, the **leader,** benefit because in owning your mistakes, you cement your personal brand as someone worthy of trust and respect. You establish a reputation of someone who communicates candidly about mistakes—not about the *person* who made the mistake. When a team or, hell, an entire organization recognizes you are genuinely focused on improvement rather than "catching" someone screw up, your followship grows. People *outside* of your team will long to work *on* your team.

I'm sure you've picked up on the fact that I feel about mistakes the same way Cousin Eddie in *Christmas Vacation* feels about the Jelly of the Month Club: they're the gift that keeps on giving—all year long. Mistakes force your operation to evolve and continuously improve.

You can't tolerate covering up mistakes and expect to have a high-performing, trusting team full of people who lean on each other—those two environments are mutually exclusive. Said plainly, owning a mistake is just the right thing to do. And remember, in a Culture of Excellence, WE do the right thing. Always.

So, where to next? Living WE 5 ensures everyone is focused on improvement, not blame. Just as important, once the mistake is on the table, the team needs to know they're surrounded by team-mates who want to help.

That's why WE pick each other up.

CHAPTER 6

WE
PICK
EACH OTHER
UP.

"

I BELIEVE THAT YOU'VE GOT TO BRING PEOPLE UP. AND IF YOU WANT SOMETHING DIFFERENT, YOU'VE GOT TO BRING THE BEST OUT OF OTHER PEOPLE. IT'S NOT JUST BRINGING THE BEST OUT IN YOU.

"

—TOM BRADY

WE 6

When I landed my first Director-level position, I was twenty-five years old, managing a team of five or six people. I was scared to death. One of my direct reports, Robert, was an older man—probably in his mid-sixties. He walked with a limp, the result of an injury suffered from one of his many tours in the Vietnam War, and was gruff and somewhat intimidating. We had very little in common, and I had problems relating to him.

After a sudden change in the quality of his work, I had to confront Robert about his performance issues, which were affecting the rest of the team. I sensed something was bothering him, but I wasn't confident enough to ask, and he wasn't the type of guy to openly share his feelings. I dreaded this conversation, but it had to be done. I delicately walked through his recent poor performance, making sure to stress how important Robert was to the team. I asked a lot of open-ended questions, trying to get to the root of the sliding performance. Robert didn't say much during the brief encounter, only sharing that both he and his wife were each dealing with health issues. I didn't push for details, but I thanked him for sharing.

At the end of our talk, Robert looked me in the eyes and said, "I respect you more than any boss I've had since leaving the military. Do you know why I respect you, Kyle?"

After an awkward coaching conversation, I certainly didn't expect a compliment. Incredulous, I could only respond with, "Why?"

"Because you look me in the eye when you talk to me, and you shook my hand at the start and end of this conversation. I realized I'm in some sort of trouble, but your approach sure helped a hell of a lot."

More than twenty years later, I still remember this exchange—in fact, I think about it often. In spite of our differences, my willingness to treat this man with the dignity and respect he deserved was enough to earn his respect in return. A handshake and eye contact, for him, resulted in a "narrowed" Leadership Gap. Using his words, Robert was indeed in "some sort of trouble." But raising my voice or ridiculing him would have done nothing to inspire improvement. At one point in his life, this man had bullets flying at him—a blustery "coaching" session from a twenty-five-year-old is laughable compared to what he's seen. Robert needed to be picked *up*, not put *down*.

When the "boss" approaches an underperforming team member as if that person is "in trouble," you can throw any chance of inspiring improvement out the window. Sure, results might improve for a short period of time—but only as a result of fear. No one should go to work with fear in their heart. It demoralizes people and leads to apathy. On the other hand, showing respect and genuine care for employees cultivates a supportive culture where people—especially the leader—look out for one another.

That's what "WE pick each other up" is all about: showing respect and care for your teammates and most importantly, having their back. When someone stumbles, the leader and other members of the team must have their arms extended, hands out, to help pick them up. You rally around that person, reminding them of their value and importance. This doesn't mean you shouldn't be tough on a *pattern* of poor results. It means you acknowledge each person's humanity through empathy and encouragement. A team committed to picking each other up ensures each person feels safe to show up to work as their authentic self. When "WE pick each other up" is part of the daily lexicon, people will trust they can risk boldly, engage fully, and feel truly connected to the rest of the team.

There are two elements to WE pick each other up. They are of equal importance and must be embraced in this order:

1. WE pick each other up in times of adversity, a misstep, or poor performance.

2. WE lift each other to new heights when we need to be rallied.

Both are necessary to create the kind of work environment where everyone not only does their jobs—they also thrive. Of course, this is not a revolutionary concept. Many companies wax poetic on the benefits of a thriving team environment. But rarely do leaders make it a priority and topic for everyday conversation. Why not?

For Me to Win, Someone Has to Lose, Right?

Why are so many still resistant to the idea of picking each other up? Once again, the chief culprit is a lack of self-confidence—fear that lifting others up minimizes one's own accomplishments or is a sign of weakness. This insecurity is self-defeating and unproductive—but doesn't change the fact that many people in the corporate world still suffer from it.

Here are just a few of the ugly ways the "me, not WE" mentality manifests.

Gotta Look Better Than My Peers

When one of my peers fails, I naturally look more competent and capable to my boss. Therefore, I'm more valuable to the company. Right?

It's this "everybody for themselves" paradigm that contributes to Corporate America's bullshit reputation. Pull yourself up by your own bootstraps; make your own luck; kill or be killed. The me-orientation guides most people to look out for themselves and themselves alone—automatically framing coworkers as competition. But there can be no real, sustained success without teamwork.

When you work *with* your peers—recognizing each person for the value they bring to the team instead of competing against each other—you unlock potential for incredible outcomes. If you support them and lift them up as a normal, everyday course of business, your goodwill is returned exponentially.

And when the leader sets this example, there is no limit to what can be achieved.

> There can be no real, sustained success without teamwork. When you work with your peers—recognizing each person for the value they bring to the team instead of competing against each other—you unlock potential for incredible outcomes.

Gotta Keep Myself Above *Them*

But what about the team you lead? They need to see you as the "leader," so you're supposed to keep distance from them, right?

It's this mindset that *creates* the Leadership Gap, thinking in zero-sum terms: if I lift others up, I shift the spotlight away from myself.

If I tip my hat to them or give any of my employees too much attention or energy—my boss sees me as less valuable.

Bosses lacking self-confidence mistakenly think they will appear to be expendable if they lift up team members. Sure, it's nice to talk about coaching people up—but not to the point they could *replace* you. Better to hold on to your position of authority, only shifting the spotlight to the team when convenient—throwing them a bone from time to time. This of course, assumes there's a finite amount of success and spotlight to go around.

Many bosses think they've *got* to protect their authority by having all the answers—if not, the team might question how they even got the job. They feel pressure to establish themselves as experts: the know-all, be-all, end-all.

Authentic leaders know better. They know being vulnerable— admitting you're far from perfect and don't have all the answers— is about as authentic as one can be. The truth is, when your team shines, you shine. The team's success endorses the leader as, well, a good leader—opening doors for the leader's growth opportunities as well as high-achieving members of the team.

> The team's success endorses the leader as, well, a good leader—opening doors for the leader's growth opportunities as well as high-achieving members of the team.

I Don't Care Anyway

In a me-oriented culture, people are so concerned about their own performance, they're too drained of energy to extend genuine care to people around them. Work friendships still happen, but close relationships are the exception rather than the rule. It's tough to pick someone up if you don't even care they've fallen. It's even tougher to build a Culture of Excellence with this mindset.

While a lot of bosses profess to "live" the stodgy, outdated mission statement that exists in most companies, they miss the opportunity to genuinely connect with their teams because that mission statement can't *force* them to legitimately care for their team. It doesn't require them to ask real questions of their employees about how they're doing or what they need. It doesn't *make* them ask, "Marissa, what do you want to do next in your career? Do you have any interest in assuming my role someday?" or, "Samantha, what's your passion? What matters most to you right now?" A "boss" doesn't care to ask those questions.

A leader *loves* to ask those questions.

It takes time and effort to pick someone up. But more importantly, it takes genuine care for those in your orbit—and many bosses don't see the potential return on the investment. As I covered in WE 3, we're all busy enough just trying to get our own work done. How are we going to find the time or the motivation to reach out and help someone else?

The fact is, a boss who wants to be elevated above all and look better than others sends the message they don't give a rat's ass about who you are or what motivates you. Are you going to deliver your best work in that environment?

It's unlikely you'll ever read the word *care* in a leadership position's job description. But if you don't care, you can't lead. Period.

When the team sees and feels how much you care about them, first as a human, and second as a professional, they work harder and more collaboratively. When they sense your commitment to them, their work is done out of passion and an equal amount of care for you. Gone are the feelings of fear, obligation, and ass-kissing. Your investment of time and attention has the potential to transform members of your team as well as the outcomes they deliver.

> If you don't care, you can't lead. Period.

A Dream Team

For the crew to wholeheartedly embrace the 10 WEs, they must be assured there will be a hand extended to them *when*—not *if*—they fall. Consider:

- For your team to do the right thing (WE 1), they must know their leader will pick them up if there's blowback from making a tough but appropriate decision.

- When you lead by example (WE 2), picking others up when they stumble, your team does the same. Not only will they pick one another up; they will also extend a hand to you— picking you up as well.

- For your team to do what they say they're going to do and follow through on commitments (WE 3), there must be an environment where people genuinely care about one another's success as well as the team's brand.

- For your team to take action and risk making a mistake (WE 4), they must know they've got the support of their leader and teammates.

- For your team to own their mistakes so problems can be solved (WE 5), they must know someone's going to pick them up rather than beat them over the head when they're most vulnerable.

Embracing WE 6 unlocks courage—the team aspires to be great, cares more, and thus tries harder. Because they know a misstep won't result in criticism and shame, the team will take calculated risks to drive improvement. The result is better outcomes delivered by passionate employees who care for one another *and* the overall team's success.

Trust me: it's a hell of a lot of fun leading in this environment. Here's why.

Colleagues Become Friends—Friends Become Family

In every job I've ever had, there were certain aspects of the role I didn't love. That's probably true for most people. From the bureaucracy that comes with working inside enormous companies to serving a boss who is impossible to please, navigating through frustrating elements of Corporate America can be a tricky thing. Many years ago, in one particularly challenging role, my boss seemed to take pride in treating me like a human punching bag. When I joined the company, I was duly warned to expect irrational and unfair criticism as standard protocol. After a few months of almost daily floggings, I questioned if this was the right gig for me. Exasperated and at my most vulnerable, I confided in a senior leader on my team who had more than a decade of experience working with my boss. I asked her, "You and the rest of the team have dealt with this behavior for so many years—why do you guys *do* this?"

"Because we love our team," she said.

Huh? Makes for a good T-shirt, but I was unconvinced. I had to be missing something. So I asked other members of my team. They all gave different takes but essentially had the same response: "We do it for each other."

And with each additional person I asked, my initial reaction of, "This is so fucking corny," evolved into the realization they really do have genuine love for each other. *That's* why they stick around and stick together. Eventually, I came to feel the love as well. Because of my affection for that team, I stayed in the role as long as I did.

A few years later, I was approached with a career move that was too good to pass up, and I made the tough decision to leave the team. Throughout my career, I made a habit of sharing big announcements, both good and bad, firsthand, with as many members of the organization as practical. Announcing my resignation was no different. During the meeting in which I announced my departure, I wept. I couldn't help it. We had become a family—warts and all—and I was sad to leave my family behind.

People stay longer and work harder when they love their team, and a supportive team inspires everyone to perform at their best. When people feel cared for and connected to one another, they face all challenges together with an open mind and a better attitude—delivering better outcomes.

All for One, One for All

During my time at that nameless company, there's a story that personifies how tightly connected a team can become and how picking each other up becomes part of the team's DNA.

A senior leader on my team was dealing with a number of personal crises, requiring her to reduce her hours and miss days altogether from time to time. When she called to fill me in, it was obvious she was under a lot of stress. I didn't want her work obligations to contribute additional stress—so I and other members of the team (her peers and direct reports) recognized we needed to shoulder the load while she was tending to the family.

The team didn't just offer hollow words of support; they essentially took ownership of many of their beloved colleague's responsibilities. We had regular check-ins to align on who was overseeing what. Her direct reports took on leading meetings she normally facilitated, while her peers took over providing me updates on her business unit's performance and in-flight initiatives. None of this activity came from my direction; the team had internalized an ethos of "WE pick each other up" and made the adjustments needed to rally around their leader. Naturally, absorbing the work of this senior leader with thousands of employees in her organization, meant everyone around her had to work harder and longer.

No one questioned how long the situation would last or how *they* would benefit from the extra effort. They did it for the love of their teammate and the team. The band played on—never missing a single beat. This leader had instilled such a strong team dynamic, she never feared what might happen if the spotlight shifted. Because, indeed, it *did* shift while she was out. But the shine illuminated talent that set the table for future leadership and growth opportunities.

This "all for one" paradigm is often nothing more than corporate rhetoric. But when you are surrounded by a team that cares enough to pick each other up, it's standard operating procedure.

Picking each other up unleashes courage and bonds the team through thick and thin. Having each other's back is a needed ingredient for building a Culture of Excellence.

Let's talk about practical ways to build and sustain a "WE pick each other up" culture.

When It's Time to Extend a Hand

I've mentioned this before, but it's worth reiterating: a title doesn't make a leader. In other words, you don't have to be responsible for a *single* direct report to be a leader. And leaders, not titles, pick people up.

On that note, let's move on to a systematic yet simple approach leaders can use when picking people up—the 5R Method. Just like the hand has five fingers extended when picking someone up, this method has five elements, all beginning with the letter *R*.

1. Recognize
2. Reaffirm
3. Remediate
4. Reduce
5. Reassess

There is one prerequisite for using the 5R Method: *care*. There is simply no way to authentically pick up someone in a time of need if you don't, on the most fundamental of levels, care for them.

1. Recognize

As soon as you recognize a team member needs support, whether they've directly indicated the need or a performance issue has gotten your attention, discuss it candidly and without judgment. For example, if a member of the team who is responsible for managing a complex project has fallen significantly behind schedule, don't sugarcoat or dance around the issue. And also, don't address it via email. Using email as a way to pick up a team member is hollow and subliminally implies they and the issue aren't terribly important.

Ideally, connect with the team member in person or, as a next best option, via video conference. A productive introduction to the conversation might sound like, "Kevin, I had a chance to review your latest project update, and if I'm reading it right, we've fallen behind schedule. Can we spend a few minutes talking through what's driving the delays?"

In this approach, I've jumped right to the topic but didn't lead with criticism or scrutiny. By saying, "If I'm reading it right," I've left the door open for Kevin to own the issue in the first breaths of the conversation. Kevin has two possible responses. He can either confirm my concern by saying, "Yeah Kyle, you're reading it right; we are behind," or he has the freedom to clarify, "Actually it's not as bad as it might seem. Here's why."

Giving the team member an opportunity to be heard first narrows the Leadership Gap and sets a collaborative, not combative, tone.

This unassuming approach puts Kevin at ease, but more importantly, the way the introduction was framed allows him to drive the conversation rather than being preached at or scolded.

Kevin and I are now in position to talk through the specifics of the issue. *How* you approach the team member has a direct impact on how transparent and forthcoming they will be in return. In the course of our conversation, Kevin acknowledges, "Yeah Kyle... Honestly, I just haven't been holding my team accountable to their goals. They're slacking off, but it's really because I haven't been managing them to keep up with the project schedule."

Recall, from WE 5, there are three kinds of mistakes: carelessness, malice, or good faith. In Chapter 5, I also covered ways to identify root causes. In this example, Kevin's project has fallen behind out of carelessness—he hasn't kept a tight oversight of competing priorities.

Once you've recognized the situation and engaged the team member, you're ready for the second *R*.

2. Reaffirm

The concern is now on the table, but before jumping to solutions, a WE-oriented leader takes a moment to reaffirm their commitment to the team member, making sure they know they're an important ingredient to the team's success. Communicate to your team member that, even though they're struggling, you remain committed to their growth and success.

Kevin's response clarified that this issue is the result of simple carelessness—Kevin needs motivation.

That motivation comes when I reaffirm my commitment to Kevin, saying something like, "Man, I appreciate you being so open and transparent with me. You know how important this project is—which is why I knew you were the right person for the job from day one. So now we're here, and I need you to know I still think you're the right person and I'm committed to making sure you succeed... so *we* succeed."

Some might be reading this and thinking, "Why the kid gloves?"

If I'm genuinely committed to Kevin, I don't want there to be any ambiguity. You see, if a team member senses a "fall from grace," they're not only dealing with the stress caused by the performance issue, but now they've got the added stress of falling out of favor with their leader. I'd rather have Kevin focused on righting the ship instead of spending energy trying to get back in my good graces.

At this point in the conversation, we've cut to the heart of the issue: I've given Kevin the opportunity to share the root cause, and he knows I have his back.

Now it's time to shift to Remediation mode.

3. Remediate

Kevin and I are aligned on what's caused the project to fall behind schedule: he's failed to keep an eye on upcoming milestones and hasn't managed his team to agreed-upon dates within the project plan. Now we need to discuss what's being done to remediate the behind-schedule project. Just like when we were in the Recognition stage, it's vital that I listen more than I talk. I need to give Kevin the opportunity to share what he's already done, in terms of remediation. If I sense he doesn't have a firm grasp on a plan of recovery, I'll diplomatically insert my thoughts on appropriate actions for improvement. Again, I want to keep the focus on the issue, not on Kevin. This is especially true during Remediation. Unless facing a pattern or a habitual performance issue, the leader should focus on what went wrong, the steps taken to ensure there won't be any repeats, and by when the train will be back on the track.

Disclaimer: since Kevin and I are discussing a complex project, it's likely there are several root causes driving the delays—each needing to be addressed. If the nature of the issue is simple and is likely to be a one-time phenomenon, you can skip the Remediation and go straight to Reassess. In other words, there's probably no remediation to be done if the issue was the result of something unavoidable or an anomaly. For example, let's say Kevin's project is behind because one of his key programmers fell ill and missed a week of work. Other than potentially discussing contingency plans, there isn't a "break" to fix.

Most "pick each other up" conversations fall into this category. A team member has stumbled and just needs encouragement or motivation. However, if there are more significant issues to resolve, go to the fourth *R*.

4. Reduce

In many ways, a leader's job is similar to an air traffic controller (ATC for short). But instead of controlling the traffic of planes in and out of the airport, the leader controls the amount and type of work to distribute to each member of the team. When a plane enters the airspace of the airport, the ATC guides them to the appropriate runway. Likewise, when work comes to the team, the leader assesses each team member's bandwidth and skill before guiding the work to the appropriate team member. Picking up a member of the team might require the leader to slow down, temporarily at least, the workload directed at a certain team member.

In this scenario, now that Kevin and I are aligned on his plan of remediation, we need to be open and realistic that something else on his plate may need to be temporarily de-prioritized and/or temporarily shifted to another team member.

I want to stress the word *temporarily* in the previous sentence.

Part of picking up a team member will often include lightening their load long enough for them to get back on track. Assuming you've done a good job playing ATC, meaning each member of the team is carrying an equal amount of weight, it's unlikely (and wouldn't be fair) to disproportionately spread assignments indefinitely because one member of the team isn't pulling their fair share.

But this is the inherent beauty of a Begin With WE culture, one where this WE is "lived" every day. If the leader is clear about *why* a decision for work reallocation is being made, focusing on the issue, not the person, the team member who is being asked to temporarily take on additional work understands the "ask" is:

1. Not indefinite
2. Required to pick up a teammate

Number 1 is incredibly important because too many times work gets piled on the best performers because, well, *they are* the best performers. This is an issue as old as the first team ever created—the best on the team, get "rewarded" for being the best by getting more work dumped on them. What's the incentive to be great there? However, if your best team member is assured this reassignment is only temporary, they're more likely to rally than become demoralized.

Number 2 is important for the same reasons I illustrated earlier in this chapter, when I shared the story about a member of my team who was thoroughly picked up while she dealt with family health issues. The team bent over backward when they knew a fellow team member was struggling. They took great pride in representing her in her absence. The point here is that a Culture of Excellence really can enable colleagues to become friends—even family. And WE look out for family.

5. Reassess

At this point, if you've followed the first four *R*s closely, you've successfully picked up a team member! You were courageous enough to have what some might consider a tough conversation. You were empathetic enough to be clear about your commitment to them. And you were open to hearing their plans to get back on track, all of which was done from a place of genuine care. You and the team member are aligned on a path to improvement. They feel empowered to improve with their self-esteem intact.

But there is one final *R* on the to-do list: *Reassess*. Reassess whether the issue was resolved and if the temporarily reallocated work can shift back to the person you picked up (and away from the awesome teammate who pitched in). You can make this a somewhat formal process by establishing a date for checking in with the team member to jointly assess progress. Or, less formally, schedule a reminder to reassess yourself.

Using Kevin and his delayed project as the example, I would reassess actual progress vs. what we discussed. I've worked with Kevin long enough to know he's a badass and he's likely to get back on schedule. He needs a motivational kick in the pants, and once he gets that, he'll be fine. (If, on the other hand, Kevin had a history of underperformance, I would be more formal in coaching him, getting explicit about the success criteria, the timing of our next check in, and the implications of continued failure.) It's my job to thank both Kevin, for his efforts, and his teammates, who picked up some of his responsibilities (temporarily).

Still not convinced? Admittedly, if you're accustomed to operating in a typical corporate environment, this might be a tough WE to buy into. The best way to overcome that skepticism? Pick up a team member. Just try it. Do it authentically, with genuine care, and it will be noticed by the entire team (especially the person you picked up). Seeing is believing.

When the team *feels* their leader is in their corner, ready to pick them up, they are much more eager to pick one another up as well.

But it's not enough to only pick up a team member when they stumble, simply getting them back to a stable level. A great leader helps them get to the *next* level.

Can You Take Them Higher?

A WE-oriented leader empowers others by creating an environment that stretches talents and ignites a passion for excellence. In other words, it's not enough to have an outstretched hand to pick up a team member who has fallen. You've got to lift them up and propel them forward. Whether you're conducting initial onboarding, managing day-to-day interactions, or meeting one-on-one or with the entire team, good leaders consistently focus on lifting up their people.

> It's not enough to have an outstretched hand to pick up a team member who has fallen. You've got to pick them up and propel them forward. Good leaders also consistently focus on lifting up their people.

We're talking about this component of WE 6 secondarily because if you don't pick others up when they need a helping hand, you certainly can't play a role in propelling them to new heights.

Hopefully this is obvious: if I make Aaron feel like a dipshit when he makes a mistake, even my best efforts to help him achieve more come across as hollow and inauthentic. Since I didn't show genuine care for his well-being and success when he needed it most, he'll never think I sincerely care about his overall growth and career path.

Making demands of people without showing them respect or consideration might get tasks accomplished, but that kind of management style is antithetical to the 10 WEs. It widens the Leadership Gap and will make people afraid to risk or try. The way to get the best out of your people is to reassure them, "Hey, on this team, WE pick each other up." By establishing a reputation for picking up a struggling team member, the leader shows they have the team's best interests at heart.

Lift *One* Up

Part of lifting others to new heights requires the leader to understand what that new height looks like for each team member. And of course the ultimate destination is specific to each member of the team. Maybe Brandon sees himself as your successor, while Jaye is quite content in her current role. And perhaps Heidi is looking to try her hand in a completely different area of the company. By the way, even and especially if Heidi is a high-performing team member, a WE-oriented leader still does their best to help her realize her next height. Anything else demonstrates you care more about your team's outcomes than those who make up the team. It's incumbent on the leader to help each team member be their best in the current role, always with an eye on helping them get to the next one. That's the right thing.

And there is only one foolproof way for identifying what team members value the most—you simply have to ask. Ask them about their passions, what matters most to them; ask if there is there anything you can do to help advance either. You're looking to find out how you can help your people be better—not just in the workplace, but in life.

Lift *All* Up

Asking the team for direct feedback is a microcosm of a larger "pick each other up" strategy. While asking questions of your direct reports is invaluable, it's also important to bring your curiosity to the macro level. This requires you to keep a pulse on what policies, approaches, and processes they find easy or difficult. The leader needs to hear what stands in the way of them being their best. You can't fix what you don't know is broken—so ask. There's tremendous goodwill fostered when the leader shows direct interest in what matters most to the team.

Assess your environment by asking questions along these lines:

- Are there topics I'm *not* covering that would be helpful to hear about?

- Do you have the resources you need to do your job effectively?
- Are you hearing enough from me on the strategy as a company?
- Are you hearing enough from me on the progress of X, Y, and Z initiatives?

Determine where *they* are and how to meet them there. Once you understand the context of where your people are today, you are more equipped to support them, lifting them higher for tomorrow.

In my consulting practice, working with leaders looking to transform their company's culture, I ask a lot of questions. One of my standard icebreaker questions is, "Tell me about your employee engagement. How's the workplace culture?"

> Once you understand the context of where your people are today, you are more equipped to support them, lifting them higher for tomorrow.

I usually get happy-talk answers, implying the culture is "fine." But regardless of how glowing or dark the response is, my follow-up question is exactly the same every time: "How do you know? Do you ask the team directly?"

This question often results in a blank stare that says, "D'oh, that's so obvious, why didn't I think of that?" The lesson here: if you want to know something from someone or a group—just ask.

Asking can be as easy as doing an employee-engagement survey—
a wonderful litmus test to help identify ways you (the leader) can
lift the team up.

An employee-engagement survey doesn't have to be overly complex; it can even be homegrown. I like to start small, with focused
statements, to have respondents gauge whether they agree or disagree. I like to use a Likert scale for responses—giving five options
ranging from "Strongly Disagree" to "Strongly Agree."

Here are some sample statements aimed at assessing if and to what
degree you are lifting the team up:

- My work gives me a feeling of personal accomplishment.
- I have the tools and resources I need to be my very best
  at work.
- My supervisor is committed to quality.
- My supervisor is committed to my professional growth.
- Our company does an excellent job keeping employees
  informed about matters affecting us.
- I can see myself working here in two years.
- My team lives the 10 WEs.
- I feel comfortable approaching management with
  suggestions or even criticism.

After you've administered the survey, benchmark the first set of
results and share the data with your teams, with no filtering—give
the good, the bad, and the ugly. This transparency removes any

bias and directs everyone to the areas needing attention. For those areas, set a goal to quantify the progress desired. For example, if only 50 percent of the respondents "Agree" their "supervisor is committed to their professional growth," work to establish a goal north of 50 percent for the next survey. From here, the leadership team develops action plans to address problematic areas. Those action plans should culminate with another survey—but allow for time for actions within the plan to take hold.

When putting new strategies in place, be overt about the action steps and consistently update the team on the efficacy of tactics and how progress is going. Remember the importance of follow-through: failing to keep the team updated has negative consequences because it tells the team it's only lip service rather than a real effort to improve things. The team needs to *feel* and *see* your dedication to lifting them up.

People often say employee engagement is difficult to measure, making it hard to get funding for assessments and remediation activity. Many executives even claim there's no ROI on such expenses. I say bullshit.

Employee engagement can be measured using employee-centric metrics like turnover, productivity, absenteeism, and of course, surveys. Every time you improve something within the work environment, you see a return on investment while lifting people up.

Cultivate a Supportive Culture

Imagine you're in an escape room with some of your best friends. If you beat that escape room with seconds to spare, do you just somberly say, "Well, um, congrats, everyone. Good work, I guess," and then awkwardly nod at each other?

Hell no! You high-five, fist-bump, and hug each other, because that's part of how we celebrate victories.

Physical touch is an incredibly valuable technique for expressing care for those in our sphere: we hold hands when we're scared, touch arms, fist-bump to show solidarity, or hug each other. Even the "elbow bump," in these pandemic days, has become a friendly gesture.

These physical points of connection are basic human responses communicating care and support, and they deserve a place in corporate culture. Of course, I realize there's a line between what's acceptable with friends and family and what's acceptable in the work environment. But fist bumps and high fives aren't much different than handshakes, and there's a real correlation between physical touch and team dynamics.

UC Berkeley conducted a study of NBA teams that measured the number of physical touches between teammates—everything from high fives, to shoulder pats, to hugs. The study found teams who touched each other the most scored more points and won more games, even after accounting for other factors like player status and early performance in the season.[12] They found that teams gain an advantage through "coded cooperative behaviors" formed through fist bumps, head grabs, team huddles, and other forms of touch.

I want that for my teams too. So when we're in person, I'll fist-bump. I'll high-five. Hell, in video calls, I'll literally put my hand or fist up to the camera and encourage others to do the same. I felt a little silly the first time I did it. But after doing it a few times, it became a normal part of our virtual meetings.

If it brings people closer, who cares if it's corny? Find your version of the fist bump. Sometimes the corny moments strengthen the team's bond and shrink the Leadership Gap.

These are powerful approaches to communicate care and support for your people. This approach shows the team you want to see them, know them, help them, and lift them to new heights. When people feel picked up in this way, they climb to those great heights.

You've Signed Up for a Marathon, Not a Sprint

I've talked about the importance of picking each other up and the benefits that come with a supportive and caring team dynamic.

12   Michael W. Kraus, Cassey Huang, and Dacher Keltner, "Tactile Communication, Cooperation, and Performance: An Ethological Study of the NBA," Emotion 10, no. 5 (2010): 745–49, https://doi.org/10.1037/a0019382.

But—*but but but*—there's a giant disclaimer for WE 6. You can't just show up one day as a leader and say, "This is how we're doing things now! Trust me; I've got your back," followed by your best version of "Kumbaya," and expect the team to be on board. In fact, taking that approach would most certainly result in understandable skepticism.

It won't work. They won't believe you. A culture of true goodwill, care, and support isn't a light switch; you can't just flip it to "on," pat yourself on the back, and say, "Mission accomplished!" Building a culture of trust and support takes time—a lot of time. Your actions speak much louder than your words, and your consistency on this front is critical.

Picture WE 6 surrounded by flashing lights and caution tape. The warning is clear: half-assing this principle will set you back beyond repair—so implement methodically and with great care. Put in the time and effort. Your vulnerability narrows the Leadership Gap and sets the example for others to follow. Seeing is believing, and for the crew to embrace this principle, they must see you live it first, especially during tough times.

Before you launch this WE, make sure you're prepared to see it through; otherwise, the skeptics will have a feeding frenzy. Your reputation to date dictates the amount of scrutiny you'll face, meaning if you've historically led with an iron fist—well, you've got a lot of work to do to prove WE 6 isn't some "unicorns-and-rainbows" happy-talk you learned from a leadership book, but don't really believe.

My advice: be hypervigilant looking for the first opportunity to pick up a team member. They will be looking too. If you don't respond with an outstretched hand and empathy, your Culture of Excellence is DOA.

No pressure, right? But the work will pay off. If you've made the effort to establish this WE among your team, when you fall short, your team will help pick you up too.

Need a Hand, Give a Hand

For the team to realize its full potential, each person must have a genuine connection with their peers and leader—a fancy way to say you *must* have "team spirit." The only way to cultivate this spirit is to model it yourself, leading by example. There is no substitution for leading with courage, vulnerability, and authenticity—no matter the circumstances. Sometimes all it takes is a handshake and eye contact—but don't be afraid to offer more. When the missteps and screwups occur, be transparent and supportive. Work to protect the morale of the person who stumbled, focusing on the opportunity, not the person. Show the team you're focused on *their* best interests, not their mistakes.

That's the beauty of an environment in which leaders and team members alike pick each other up. Whether picking your people up when they need a hand, or in lifting them to new heights, the leader's job is to inspire the team to reach its highest and best potential. And in turn, the team inspires you to be a better leader *for them,* because you've inspired them in ways they likely haven't previously felt in the workplace.

This sets us up for WE 7: WE measure ourselves by outcomes. Not activity.

CHAPTER 7

WE

MEASURE OURSELVES

BY OUTCOMES.

NOT ACTIVITY.

"
DON'T MISTAKE ACTIVITY FOR ACHIEVEMENT.
"

—JOHN WOODEN

WE 7

Early in my career, I ran a department that was responsible for producing and disseminating a bevy of production reports. It was during this time that I learned two important things about operational reporting:

1. The level of effort that goes into enterprise reporting can be astounding.
2. The number of people who don't even read the reports—even custom reports designed specifically *for* them—is astonishing.

It never failed: report recipients routinely asked my group questions about data that was in a published report—meaning they hadn't read it. We already knew they hadn't because our reporting software informed us who had or hadn't opened each report.

When I came to Maximus, I was overwhelmed with the volume of reports produced by our Reporting and Analytics group. I talked to John Campbell, who ran the department, and learned his team produced *583* reports—a mix of daily, weekly, monthly, and quarterly. John readily agreed the sheer volume of reports generated was excessive.

That's a lot of information being shared, and the data within all those reports is key for making sound operational decisions. But there are problems with so much reporting too.

First, how many of those reports added real value? Sure, some of them were consumed daily and helped inform leaders. But of the 583 produced, how many were really arming the team with not just data but *information* that contributed to a delighted customer or improved the employee experience? In truth, it was simply impossible to tell. This was akin to the old philosophical thought experiment: If a tree falls in a forest and no one is around to hear it, does it make a sound? If a report is generated for years and no one consumes it, is it needed?

What's worse, with so many reports being generated, the likelihood of an error increased exponentially, leading to inconsistency across reports. As a result, we were either getting bad information or losing time playing the reporting equivalent of *Where's Waldo?*—trying to figure out which report was accurate. I recall multiple instances of trying to make sense of two different reports with the same data field but with different values.

I had a lot of questions for John. But mostly, the questions took varying forms of *why*: "Why is this report done so often? Why do we even have this report? Why isn't this report consolidated with that report? And why don't these two numbers match?!"

After John, a hell of a smart guy, answered all of my questions, I entered classic Kyle mode: I got the top dozen operations and reporting people into a room, and we went through every single report. We critically analyzed which reports were essential and which could be eliminated and/or consolidated. When we were done, we'd eliminated hundreds of reports.

It's difficult to blame any one person for this reporting clusterfuck. It wasn't John's or his team's fault—they are incredibly smart and were basically "filling" orders requested by the Operations team. In defense of John's team, even they were skeptical of how many reports were actually being consumed but hadn't been given permission to winnow their activity down.

The *activity* required to design and deliver a huge percentage of those reports had very little, or nothing at all, to do with driving our *outcomes*.

This classic example highlights two typical outcomes when an organization isn't purposeful on policing its activities, ensuring each and every one of them is connected to an outcome.

First is the unfortunate fact that John's team was tied up, spinning its wheels, delivering a portfolio of reports—a portfolio more than double the size it needed to be. In other words, up to *half* of this team's activity was wasted time.

The second outcome is related: since the team was engaged in useless activities, they were "too busy" to take on work that *was* connected to outcomes—work that would have provided a greater sense of fulfillment and meaning to the team's workday.

That, my friends, is not the recipe for building a Culture of Excellence.

This is why WE measure ourselves by outcomes, not activity.

Outcomes, Activities, and You

Before we get too far, let's align on some simple definitions for these two terms. **Outcomes** are generally measurable and are the *end result*—representing the "what" in the equation. **Activities** are the tactics used to achieve the outcome—representing the "how" in the equation.

> Outcomes are generally measurable and are the end result—representing the "what" in the equation. Activities are the tactics used to achieve the outcome—representing the "how" in the equation.

Show Me the ~~Money~~ Outcomes

Because everyone in Corporate America is *so* busy, when I deliver a Begin With WE keynote, I often see looks of confusion when I get to WE 7. Most folks in the audience appear to take exception to the idea that their busy day doesn't exclusively drive outcomes.

However, I like to frame it this way: outcomes are what the company delivers in order to make money. Customers don't pay for the activity required to deliver the outcome.

Taking this bottom-line perspective is a helpful way to differentiate activity from outcome. However, I still get frustrated when activities are presented as outcomes in the workplace. For instance, let's say I ask for an update on an agreed-upon deliverable from a member of my crew, Sandra:

"Sandra—last week, we agreed you would bring our YTD facilities spend to today's meeting. Whatcha got?"

Too often, I get answers like, "Oh yes, I'm on it! I have a meeting scheduled with Jim in finance."

I tend to have a visceral reaction to this answer. Sandra's telling me about an *activity*—one that I don't particularly need or want to know about. (Especially since the activity hasn't even taken place yet, and the number is due now.) Lauding that she's scheduled a meeting is like my Uber driver looking for praise because he stopped for gas before his shift. I'm glad Sandra has taken the initiative to get with the right person to get the number, but I am no closer to the outcome than I was a week ago.

This is where many go astray. They say, "I did this" or "I did that," listing activities they've mistaken as outcomes. And they feel like their activity should be recognized on some level *as* an outcome.

However, nothing's been accomplished. Don't tell me about your activity or busywork. Tell me about your *outcomes.*

Activities Are Important Too

While it's true, the customer doesn't pay for (and usually doesn't care about) the activity necessary to achieve an outcome, activities are indeed important—so long as they're easily connected to an outcome. If you can't draw a clear connection from an activity to a specific outcome, it's probably not important. In fact, it's probably getting in the way of something else that *is* directly connected to an outcome, which could use more time and attention.

Disclaimer: I've been careful to use qualifiers like **usually, probably,** *or* **often** *because if I were reading this book, I'd be the first one jumping up to say, "Bullshit, I can think of an activity that doesn't directly connect to an outcome, but it's totally important." Without question, exceptions exist—for example, activities related to maintaining compliance may not impact the customer directly but are still necessary. However, those are the exceptions that prove the rule.*

If it doesn't advance or add value to the company, the client, and/or the crew, it's probably unnecessary activity.

Simple Enough—But Why the Confusion?

If we agree outcomes matter most and activities are needed to enable those outcomes, why do so many cultures get it wrong? There are two primary culprits driving the confusion. First, because activities are generally easier to complete, the sense of accomplishment that comes with completion has a way of bolstering the ego, making us feel as if we've added value. This makes sense but can't be addressed without recognizing number two: the temptation to shrug and say, "It's just how we do things here."

Activity Makes People Feel Important

It feels good to be productive. Racing from meeting to meeting, running reports, and building presentations is a pretty typical day for many in Corporate America. You've been so "busy," when the day wraps, it feels like you've earned your paycheck.

Since you were also a significant contributor in all those meetings, you no doubt are left with an impression of importance. Ironically, as your stress level and weariness increase—like when you're double-booked—your sense of importance increases too. And with all the "multitasking" (replying to emails or texts while in meetings, checking email while in 1:1s, for example), there's no way you're giving full attention to any one of those activities—but you're exhausted. That counts for something, right?

Indeed, activity *is* exceptionally important—it's how the sausage is made. But the satisfaction and sense of importance that comes with accomplishing an activity can go too far and become habitual.

Because that packed calendar provides a sense of importance and you're zapped at the end of the day, it's understandably hard to admit a lot of your activity is meaningless. Or at least meaningless as it relates to outcomes that drive the business or employee engagement. If you call a client and say, "Hey, Ms. Consumer, I spent eight hours in meetings today!" you'll find Ms. Consumer doesn't give a shit—because your activity doesn't matter if it has no connection to the product or service she buys.

Just mathematically speaking, there are typically multiple activities per outcome, making the number of chances to conflate activities and outcomes even greater (and even more understandable). We want to reward the team for their contributions. But giving out "participation ribbons" for valueless activities leads to confusion about what sort of action is truly worthwhile.

> ## Activities aren't why we get paid. Outcomes are why we get paid.

But a false sense of importance isn't the only reason we can't let go of our frenzied (and potentially meaningless) activity.

It's Just How We Do Things Here

When activity is mistaken for outcome in a corporate environment, the problem is usually more widespread than a single team. It's typically ingrained in the company's cultural fabric. This is because of our competitive nature.

To illustrate the point, let's say I lead a team of sales professionals and hold them to high standards. My peer Gus runs a parallel team and it seems like he's always giving out awards and kudos for activity that—as far as I can tell—meets the basic requirements of the job. Even our boss constantly congratulates Gus for boosting his team's morale. Naturally, members of my team complain about the lack of "participation ribbons" coming their way. Feeling the pressure, I start passing out party hats and noisemakers after every cold call. And lo and behold, a company-wide culture that celebrates activity—regardless of its connection to outcomes— begins to proliferate. No one wants to be shown up by a peer who makes a living lauding their employees for trivial activities.

Believe me, I'm not minimizing the impact of employee recognition. But when the recognition is doled out for simply making the sausage, employees receive the message, "Activity *equals* productivity."

During a recent consulting effort, I was conducting an interview with a senior executive, Bradley, and the conversation turned to "bandwidth." Bradley shared that he wished there were more hours in the day because he has a hard time "getting to it all." At one point in the conversation, he rotated his laptop in my direction to show me his packed calendar. He clicked through the next several days to prove his point. Later the same day, I interviewed the head of human resources, Caroline, and I asked about "bandwidth" concerns for the senior leadership team. She chuckled and said, "Yeah, including me!" She continued, "But it's just what we do here."

This is bad folks, very bad. I was speaking with two of the most senior leaders in a multimillion-dollar company, and they treat activity as if they don't have a say in what gets attention and what doesn't. They spoke as if their calendars were preordained and they weren't able to trim the fat, so to speak. If these two were confusing activity with outcomes, it's most likely the leaders reporting to them and those deeper into the organization are operating within the same paradigm.

When "activity equals productivity," employees stop questioning the *reason* behind why they're doing the activity in the first place. When activity is an end unto itself, it must be scrutinized. Otherwise, you're wasting your team's energy and exhausting their passion for their role.

Wasted Energy

When I was working with John Campbell and team to figure out "The Mystery of Nearly Six Hundred Reports," detailed at the start of the chapter, we very literally scrutinized every single report. Quite often, the explanation behind a report went something like this: "Someone wanted *this one* because something broke six months ago, and they requested the report as a form of quality check."

"Is that thing working fine now?"

"Yes, it's totally fine."

"So...do we still need the daily quality checks?"

"Probably not; we haven't had an issue in a few quarters."

This scenario is not uncommon. Activity-driven bosses are notorious for setting up a process to address something specific for a given time, only for that process to be allowed to run in perpetuity. In fact, this is also true for meetings. Something breaks, and a leader says, "I want to make sure this is not broken every day for the next thirty days, just to make sure we've fixed it."

Good plan, in and of itself—the leader's doing the right thing, taking action, following through. Unfortunately, though, too often a leader commissions a new report to track that data and doesn't even realize that data is already tracked and available in a different report. So now we've got redundancy. That wouldn't be a huge issue if the new report was retired after thirty days—but usually, it's not.

Once "Leadership" gets the answer or reassurance they needed from the data, they'll no longer open the email or read the report. They'll forget about it and no one will think to sunset the report or question the need to continue doing the same activity. In some cases, as with several of those reports I went through with John and the team, the person who initially requested the report may not even be with the company anymore.

Trimming the fat takes courage and will be uncomfortable at first. At some point, someone needs to take a step back and ask, "Is this still needed? Is it adding value?"

That someone is you.

How to Lead the Paradigm Shift

Ideally, every activity, every meeting, every report, every QA check, etc. has a direct impact on outcomes. My earlier disclaimer regarding exceptions notwithstanding, the lion's share of activity should directly connect to an outcome that advances the standing of the company, client, and/or crew.

> Shifting the paradigm toward outcome-driven activity and away from activity for the hell of it requires a deliberate focus from you, the leader.

Let's talk about how to take your team in that direction.

Conspicuous Communication

While much of the corporate world is focused exclusively on outcomes, we need to shift to a relentless focus on *connecting activity to outcomes*. Leaders must drive the shift by conspicuously driving conversations toward outcomes and having little tolerance for disconnected activity. "Outcome-driven activity" should be part of the team's vernacular.

Remember Sandra? She scheduled time with Jim in finance. She was given a task and understandably needs help to produce the target outcome. She has no way of even getting to the outcome until she meets with Jim. In her mind, like so many others in Corporate America, scheduling a meeting is confused as but one of several outcomes needed to get the number. But in reality, it's only activity.

Yes, getting the meeting on the calendar is a *required activity* for Sandra to deliver the outcome. However, in this scenario, Sandra was given a task to complete prior to the next weekly meeting. She didn't deliver, even though her response indicates progress.

> Shift to a relentless focus on *connecting activity to outcomes*. Leaders must drive the shift by conspicuously driving conversations toward outcomes and having little tolerance for disconnected activity. "Outcome-driven activity" should be part of the team's vernacular.

That's not all on Sandra, though. The leader is responsible to be conspicuous when it comes to setting expectations for how to view activity vs. outcome. If Sandra and I were already operating in a WE-oriented paradigm, when I made the request for facilities spend, I could have gone a step further by saying something like, "I'm not sure if you have access to that number or you need to partner with someone, so you might need to jump through a few hoops to get there, but my expectation is we review the number this time next week. If for some reason that's not doable, let me know as soon as possible."

This level of explicit communication helps them, help *you*. The moral of the story: don't allow the team to confuse activity *required for* an outcome with the actual outcome itself. How you manage your team's activity, meetings included, is a game changer in terms of productivity and outcomes delivered.

> Don't allow the team to confuse activity *required for* an outcome with the actual outcome itself.

Like every WE, successfully implementing WE 7 requires you to lead by example, being transparent about how you're spending *your* time. This transparency opens the door for you to discuss how others should spend *their* time as well.

For example, if you attend a meeting that fails to advance a desired outcome, it's your obligation to share that opinion with other attendees. It's important to be open-minded. It's possible you missed the connection between the activity discussed in the meeting and the desired outcome. But if you failed to see the connection, it's possible others did as well. Your candor about how everyone on the team, including you, spends their time communicates that everyone's valuable time is limited, so we must spend it wisely.

Evangelize the Outcome Paradigm

When focusing on outcomes, leaders must transparently, emphatically, and repeatedly espouse the "why" for every major assignment, explaining *why* that activity is meaningful.

Also, make sure you attend the "right" meetings—those where an outcome has been clearly articulated in the invite—and skip those with an ambiguous purpose. For both types of meetings, communicate—again—*why* you've prioritized your time the way you have. This sends the message that you're committed to working to get shit done—not scheduling a meeting to discuss another meeting (the meeting before the meeting) that has an agenda with no clear deliverable in sight.

Here's another example of how you can model the shift. Let's say someone on my team says, "Hey, we should have a meeting with Travis and Annie to talk about _____."

I might push back and say, "Why should that be a meeting? Can we pick up the phone and call them now or send them an email with a very specific focus? What's the most efficient way to achieve that outcome?"

In many cultures, "Let's schedule a meeting" has become the de facto way to solve problems. But it doesn't have to be this way. Don't "kick the can" for a decision to be made. Doing so only creates more activity and delays the outcome.

Set Measurable Goals

Because outcomes are nearly always tangible, you should likewise set tangible, measurable, outcome-related goals for your team. This allows you to quantify results and focus on the finish line for each person. The performance appraisal shouldn't be full of happy-talk success criteria. Rather, each member of the team should have a review that includes a handful of tangible goals with quantified outcomes. Then it's your job to get out of the way and let them deliver. In other words, don't be prescriptive on *how* the team member delivers—but rather be precise on *what* is delivered.

> Don't be prescriptive on *how* the team member delivers—but rather be precise on *what* is delivered.

By definition, focusing on a finite number of quantified outcomes reduces the number of non-value-add activities. For me, having a short list of outcomes I *must* achieve during a given period pushes me to focus on the shortest path to get from here to there for each outcome. Setting measurable goals creates an expectation on where the effort should go and where it *doesn't* need to go.

Manage the Milestones

It's fairly easy to give your team members tangible, measurable goals with short-term activities. But the loftier or more complex a project or initiative, the more critical it is to conspicuously bifurcate activity from outcome. To do this, simply establish key milestones along the way to "launch."

For example: years ago, I oversaw the rollout of a new customer relationship management (CRM) platform. We were introducing a new desktop tool to over two thousand people at three different sites. This was an eighteen-month, $30+ million project, so the planning had to be tight. There were plenty of dependencies—we couldn't get to second base without rounding first base, so to speak.

The project plan itself was hundreds of pages. One could argue everything on the project plan was a description of activity and the "go live" of the CRM was the *only* outcome. Not so—there were hundreds, if not thousands, of outcomes on which to focus (and celebrate): for instance, the completion of code development, user-acceptance testing (UAT), regression testing, and so on. All of these milestones were required incremental *outcomes* of the ultimate project outcome. Additionally, the many meetings required to discuss the code, approach to UAT, and approach to regression testing were all activities leading to outcomes. Each of those meetings was directly connected to goals within the project that collectively led to launching the new technology across all sites.

The CRM would solve a whole bucket of problems for us; however, getting it launched was a bucket of problems in and of itself. Like anything else in life, we had to take that big bucket of problems and turn it into smaller buckets of problems, with each of those smaller buckets representing an outcome—a milestone. And because we'd divided the massive task into more manageable steps, we had clarity needed to fill our schedules with *just* the necessary activities that would lead to each outcome's success. By identifying those key milestones, we stayed on track, remained focused, and didn't allow unnecessary activity to distract from progress.

Tracking of milestones is also important for sustaining motivation and momentum—keeping morale high among your team. Let's take a different example. Suppose my team is working to improve customer satisfaction (CSAT) scores from an average of 70 to 80. If I say, "Hey, how are our CSAT numbers looking?" when the team's only gotten to 75, what are they going to say?

"We're still trying to get to 80, Kyle. We'll let you know when we get there."

Rather than celebrating their progress, they end up apologizing for it. That doesn't make sense.

On the other hand, if we've established incremental milestones, the team has tangible, incremental progress to make—and celebrate—along the way. Being specific about the building blocks required to reach a long-term outcome inherently sets the team up for multiple opportunities for success.

It's difficult to gauge the pace and trajectory of improvement if you haven't established goals to track progress against the ultimate outcome. However, establishing outcome-oriented, incremental milestones helps you act short-term, even while you've strategized long-term. This provides more opportunities to pass out a few prizes—not participation ribbons, mind you—but legitimate rewards for significant accomplishments.

Celebrate Progress

Staying informed and up-to-date on progress also gives you the chance to celebrate with your team as incremental outcomes are reached along the way. Celebrating progress toward the ultimate goal helps your team sustain momentum and positive morale while running the marathon. Conspicuously recognizing the achievement of short-term outcomes further drives the paradigm shift from activity to outcomes.

The subliminal benefit: celebrating the achievement of milestones during ongoing initiatives reinforces WE 7—outcomes over activity. If you're consistently less excited about activity than you are about quantified outcomes, you're setting the example for the team to operate in the same way.

The key is identifying the measurables to track and celebrate.

Be Smart about Your Metrics

The only thing as important as setting a measurable goal is choosing the right metrics to quantify progress toward or achievement of the goal.

Wrong metrics cause more confusion than clarity. For example, in the call center world, call times are measured in various ways. Almost every call center measures each employee's average handle time. Average handle time is calculated from the time the call is answered to the time you're done executing whatever action is needed to effectuate the caller's request, divided by the number of phone calls taken over a certain period of time. Ideally, we want to take care of a customer's needs as efficiently as possible, allowing us to complete more phone calls and take care of more customers.

This metric can be slippery. There's a lot of debate in the call center world about whether handle time should be a sentinel metric. When used thoughtfully, this data point can be incredibly valuable, but when taken at face value, an employee's average handle time can be misleading.

For example, if my call center has a handle time goal of ten minutes, and everyone's coming in at eight minutes, the assumption is we're killing it, right? Not so fast—in isolation, the metric doesn't tell the entire story. A more accurate picture of the call center's efficiency should include a metric for transfer-out calls. These are calls where the call center *can't* help the customer, so the caller is transferred to another department.

> The only thing as important as setting a measurable goal is choosing the right metrics to quantify progress toward the goal.

How do transfers impact our handle time? Those shorter calls make us look better. But here's the problem: employees, in an effort to stay off the radar and keep their handle time down, can inappropriately transfer callers to another department. Since "what gets measured, gets managed," the me-oriented boss may not even care about those inappropriate transfer-outs. They'll only focus on the team achieving the one metric being measured: the lowest possible average handle time.

The handle time metric, on its own, isn't an accurate picture of how efficiently we're resolving the customer's needs. Sometimes, unfortunately, we're just shuffling them around. With an incomplete set of metrics, the people reading the reports would miss that fact.

If the call center prides itself on delivering superior service, using average handle time, in isolation at least, isn't the right metric. Why? Using this metric sends the message that speed is more important than service—so employees favor rushing a caller off the phone over delivering a superior experience. A better metric would include a comparison of the average handle time alongside the numbers indicating transfer-out calls.

Make sure you're using the right data to determine whether your team's activity is achieving the desired outcome—for your team's sake *and* for the customer's benefit.

Review Progress Regularly

Finally, after you've identified desired outcomes, set both long- and short-term goals, and established the right metrics to track, you must plan to track progress.

It's irresponsible to take those first three steps and just sit back and wait until you cross the "finish line" to check for success.

Schedule check-ins throughout the team's journey and stick with them. Regular check-ins show the team you care about their work, their goals, and their outcomes. When *you're* invested in the team's success, they care more too.

If the runway between strategy and final outcome is a long one, from time-to-time competing priorities and other initiatives might distract you from diligently driving these check-ins. Your team will take notice if they sense you've taken your eye off the ball. It's human nature. And as a result, they are more likely to lose their focus as well.

This reminds me of a classic example I lived at CVS. Our Specialty Pharmacy division had a multi-month plan for modernizing self-service capabilities. I chaired the initiative's steering committee, which essentially required me to play devil's advocate on updates, and, of course, encourage and reward progress. With a program spanning many months, it's not uncommon for a steering committee meeting to be canceled occasionally. However, for this effort, I noticed about half of the meetings were either postponed or canceled altogether. When I asked for explanations for all the delays, I was given what seemed like legitimate reasons for the shifts. I allowed the cancellations to dull my focus and instead trusted the executive over the program would alert me if the team got off track.

Every now and then, she would alert me of an issue. But her alerts didn't come as frequently as the meetings were being rescheduled—leaving me confused and concerned. This finally came to a head when yet another steering committee meeting was canceled about ten minutes before it was to begin. Frustrated, I called the executive in charge and politely asked for the canceled meeting to take place as scheduled. When I joined the meeting, I simply asked why the meeting was canceled again.

The reason: the team wanted to mask the fact that critical milestones were being missed and delays were piling up. The project scorecard was bright red. The team was working to remediate the issues and ostensibly didn't want to share the bad news with me. What a shame—the meeting was canceled for the very purpose it was originally scheduled—to check in on progress and remove barriers to delivery. Because the project timeline was lengthy, I was lulled into thinking the team was on top of the situation and progressing as scheduled. I allowed the executive to gloss over her updates and lost my focus on helping drive the ultimate outcome. Needless to say, that was the last of the canceled steering committee meetings.

The leader must be diligent, consistently reviewing progress and keeping everyone's focus on the desired outcomes—and don't let them wiggle out of it.

The Meeting Monolith

Without a doubt, the biggest hurdle to wide-scale embrace of WE 7 is Corporate America's incessant reliance on meetings. Don't get me wrong; a good meeting is invaluable—but only when it's actually needed and advances progress toward an identified outcome. But far too many meetings fail to add any value whatsoever. A recent study from the highly respected international consulting firm Korn Ferry (KF), found **67 percent** of workers surveyed indicated most meetings *kept them from delivering* their best work. Only *11 percent* said all of their meetings are productive.[13]

How does this happen? Senior Client Partner at Korn Ferry, Cathi Rittelmann says it best: "Too often, the answer to any work issue is, 'Let's meet.'"

Rather than address the issue in real time, invites are sent out, and people just click "accept"—even when they're not sure if the meeting is relevant to them. In fact, the same KF study revealed *35 percent* of workers surveyed indicated they would attend a meeting even *if they believed it would not be a productive use of their time.* When the calendar alerts chime, they walk from their cubicles or log on to their Zoom to attend, even though they know they have more important things to accomplish. What a damn shame.

> 35 percent of workers surveyed indicated they would attend a meeting even if they believed it would *not* be a productive use of their time.

13   "Working or Wasting Time?" Korn Ferry, November 12, 2019, https://www.kornferry.com/about-us/press/working-or-wasting-time.

What would happen if you didn't show up? Have you ever been double-booked? Triple-booked? For most, the answer is a quick yes. So naturally, you've missed meetings from time to time. Now ask yourself: How many times did the company go bankrupt or something totally implode because you missed the meeting?

Never?

Even as a leader, when you're overbooked and miss those meetings, miraculously, your team generally finds a way to figure things out without you. The odds of major fallout from a missed meeting are slim to none—especially if you do your due diligence and check in with someone after the meeting to see if you've missed anything important.

I'm here to tell you, the wheels don't usually fall off from missing a meeting. Or two meetings.

A WE-oriented leader takes an *active* role in eliminating unnecessary meetings. Do so by challenging the organizer. Ask questions like:

- What do we hope to accomplish in this meeting?
- Could this be handled via a phone call between two people?
- Would an email work?
- Do we really need [insert name of person who has attended the last several of these recurring meetings but hasn't said a word] to attend?

- Why do we have three people from the same team here? Can't one represent the group?

Some may not appreciate this approach, but I see it differently. You're protecting your people's most valuable asset: their time.

Some meetings are truly necessary. *Some* meetings are productive. How do you know if a meeting is necessary? Generally, prior to the meeting, you can draw an imaginary line from the purpose of the meeting to an identified outcome. And likewise for the end of the meeting. However, if at the conclusion, you can't draw the line, then discuss the value of the meeting, especially if it's recurring, with the organizer. (And think seriously about not attending the next one.)

Let's go deeper.

Why Am I Here?

Admittedly, I've joined more than my share of meetings where I found myself asking this very question. The alternative and more tragic version—"Why are *we* here?"—has also crossed my mind more times than I care to remember.

This confusion is a common problem because people find safety casting a wide net and inviting too many meeting participants—essentially using the invite list as a way to cover their asses. In other words, they view the meeting as a form of communication rather than a tool to advance an outcome.

Not only is this approach lazy, but it monopolizes attendees' (those who actually come) time. And with too many people in the room, you run two risks. First, the bigger the group, the more likely many participants won't speak up and engage. As a result, they don't contribute, and important information isn't shared.

Second, the opposite happens, and *too many* people speak up. When too many people have an opinion, it's nearly impossible to make a decision or make real progress. This scenario also leads to "scope creep." The group is together to solve X, but someone mentions something about Y, shifting the conversation exclusively to Y, leaving X unsolved. But bet your ass there will be another meeting scheduled to discuss X. And of course, someone will request yet another meeting to discuss Y—and the meeting monolith grows.

So who *really* needs to be in the meeting? Take a moment to consider who is genuinely needed and who isn't. If you think someone only needs to know the outcome of the meeting, but doesn't necessarily have a dog in the fight, just make sure they get meeting minutes. But don't be so quick to invite them. As a general rule: the lower the number of people, the more productive the meeting.

Time Keeps On Ticking...

Have you ever noticed how most sixty-minute meetings seem to last, well, sixty minutes? What about thirty-minute meetings? Somehow, they also tend to last right around the scheduled duration as well.

This "coincidence" has very little to do with how clairvoyant the meeting organizer was when scheduling the meeting and a lot to do with how most of us are hardwired. As if we aren't in control of how we spend our day, we *find* ways to fill the time allotted, whether it's adding value or not. And if we run over, no problem—just schedule another meeting.

Also, what's the magic that thirty and sixty seem to hold over us? What about the fifteen-minute meetings? The forty-five-minute meetings? Every meeting doesn't have to be in a thirty-minute increment—a group of focused, task-oriented team members can knock out plenty of productive work in less.

This is not about, "Can I do sixty minutes' worth of work in thirty minutes?" or, "Can I stretch this thirty-minute conversation into sixty minutes and enjoy shooting the breeze a little?" Instead, the question to ask is, "How much time do *we really need* to accomplish the objectives of the meeting?"

As a matter of fact, you *are* in charge of how you spend your day. We've all heard meeting organizers say, "Hey, we're done early! I'm going to give you back ten minutes of your day." Cue unproductive time—usually, people end up wasting those ten minutes. Whereas if they'd been able to anticipate the correct meeting length, they might have been able to plan something productive with that extra time. The lesson: don't schedule an hour if the topic can be covered in forty-five minutes. Schedule forty-five minutes.

Limiting time isn't the only way to get more out of your meetings. Likewise, try to limit the number of slides used as well as the amount of text on each slide. PowerPoint is great for sharing data points but terrible for engagement. Instead of having a conversation, organizers/presenters simply read from their presentation "slideware." Adults don't need to be read to. In fact, when the presenter drones on, they usually aren't heard anyway because meeting participants have pressed fast-forward, skimming ahead in the deck. Granted, PowerPoints can be helpful for nervous presenters, but really, they're no substitute for knowing your shit.

Limits, my friends. Set boundaries for allotted time and slideware.

Stay the Course

I mentioned scope creep earlier. Encourage the facilitator and attendees to be purposeful about the discussion—ensuring the conversation stays within the bounds of the original scope of the meeting. It's important to know what's in scope and what's out of scope—and stay the course.

Are we meeting to solve a problem? Are we here to come up with a plan to execute a task? Everyone in the meeting should have an idea of the target outcome of the meeting; if you don't know, contact the organizer and ask, "What are we planning to accomplish?" If you *are* the organizer, the invite should leave no ambiguity as it relates to the purpose and expected outcome of the meeting.

Once you're *in* the meeting, and you sense the conversation is wandering from the meeting's original intent, a leader:

- Makes sure everyone in the meeting is aligned on the purpose and expected outcome
- Ensures the conversations stay on task
- Plays the role of timekeeper

Incidentally, this is true whether you're the facilitator or not. If you're a leader in a wandering meeting, it's your obligation to speak up and redirect, keeping people on task. If you want to be seen as a leader, you have to lead, including meetings and people that wander.

But wait—if you're doing this but you're *not* the facilitator, wouldn't you come across as a jackass? Potentially. However, the other option is to sit through a meeting that has minimal impact toward an outcome—i.e., wasting a lot of people's time. Don't want to sound like a jackass? The art is in the delivery.

When the conversation begins to drift, diplomatically redirect the dialogue back to the objective of the meeting. Do so while remaining open that others may take a different path than you might take to get to the same destination. In other words, a facilitator or attendee may think it's necessary to share information they think is relevant, even if you don't. If you've remained open and are still missing the connection, it's possible others are too—but they aren't courageous or comfortable enough to speak up. In this scenario, a diplomatic redirect might be, "It's entirely possible I'm missing something, Stacy, but can you help me understand how this relates to _____?"

If yours is the type of organization where meeting scope creep is common, consider giving some prework before facilitating the meeting. Doing so sets clear expectations for what needs to be accomplished and allows for more productive input from the group, since they've had a chance to plan ahead.

But what if the person doing the scope creep shuffle is the boss? Admittedly, I've been *"that* guy"—many times. And when I get on a roll on a topic that isn't within the guideposts of the meeting, I've had great teams who weren't afraid to speak up and say, "Hang on, Kyle—let's bring it back to X." If you have a desire to be *"that* person who gets on a roll," be open to this redirect—otherwise you widen the Leadership Gap. You can't preach the benefits of running effective meetings while occasionally using them for your personal Toastmasters project.

I understand these approaches might ruffle some feathers in the beginning. So your approach to meeting management is critical. Remind those in attendance that you're just looking out for them and this discipline is needed to protect everyone's precious time.

Keeping the meeting on course is a tricky proposition, but when you do it consistently, others notice and will begin to do the same.

Engage!

Do your best to keep meeting attendees engaged. In an environment where some might be attending in person and others are attending virtually, make sure everyone has a chance to be heard. As the facilitator, don't be afraid to randomly call on attendees directly—this is especially important for those online.

Engaging attendees sets the expectation that everyone comes to the meeting prepared and stays attentive during the conversation. If you're the one doing most of the talking, it's not a meeting—it's a speech. One person dominating the dialogue is the best way to get nothing done and ensure limited participation. Look at it from their point of view—you're the boss, so they *have* to sit and listen.

Remember, good leaders listen more than they talk. Facilitate, don't dominate.

Allow People to Skip Your Meetings

Here's another rarely considered approach to focusing on outcomes over activity. It's okay to miss meetings. Really. It would be hypocritical to condemn someone for missing a meeting if they missed it because they're working on delivering an outcome.

This approach only works in an environment that prioritizes outcomes. You're surrounded by professionals, and it's important to treat everyone as such. Each member of the team should be given the latitude to decide which priority is most deserving of their time and attention: this meeting or closing out another deliverable (outcome)?

When one of my direct reports misses a meeting, I might not even ask them about it. But if decisions were made, they'll probably have to live with them. However, if they say, "Kyle, I need a pass for this afternoon's meeting—I've got to stay focused on a report for the client. I'd like to send Juan in my place," I'll *encourage* them to miss. An outcome for a client should *almost* always take priority over anything I've asked them to attend. "Forcing" a team member to attend a meeting is a move born out of arrogance, as if to say, "I'm more important than the client." Clearly, I'm not.

Being okay with team members missing your meetings emphasizes the importance of outcomes over activity. Allow the professionals on your team to focus on what drives outcomes vs. holding them accountable to attend a meeting, just because you can.

The Straight Line

Back in my days at Optum, I worked for a good man named Andy Slavitt—a brilliant guy who played a major role in rescuing *Healthcare.gov* when the federal government struggled to launch the Affordable Care Act (Obamacare). His work garnered attention from a handful of states who were also struggling to implement their own State-Based Marketplace (the state-run version of Obamacare), and Optum started receiving calls from governors of these states—Slavitt needed help.

I'd developed a reputation as a "transformation guy," and somehow he was aware of my work within Optum. I was thrilled to be asked to lead an effort to bail out those struggling states. My team and I worked around the clock, living in hotels for months on end. We designed and implemented new processes and provided hundreds of resources to process hundreds of thousands of applications for healthcare enrollment. But not even working sixteen to twenty hours a day ("activity") would have mattered if the states couldn't process an enrollment application ("outcome"). Our efforts paid off, and the market took notice.

A Wall Street analyst wrote an article about Optum's involvement, citing us as "saviors," and our stock popped.

Slavitt emailed me the next day with a copy of that article. His message read, "It should be a proud day for you. Not many individuals can move the stock price of a multibillion-dollar company."

This was nearly eight years ago, and I still have that email. It reminds me of just how powerful and satisfying it is when your efforts lead to a meaningful outcome.

The recognition was heartwarming—not because it meant a feather in my cap, but because it was confirmation that the hard work led to important outcomes for so many citizens and therefore our company.

That's the kind of reward that comes when WE measure ourselves by outcomes, not activity.

The shortest distance between two points is a straight line. When we zigzag our way to the outcome, it usually means we either don't know the straight line or we're just engaging in activity that isn't the best use of our team's talent and time.

Are we producing redundant reports nobody's reading? Are we sitting in meetings even though we don't know why we're there? Whatever the case, if you can't draw a straight line from the activity to the desired outcome, why do it?

On the other hand—if you *can* draw the straight line, if the meetings you attend are productive and meaningful, if the work you're doing has a measurable impact for the company, client, or crew— you should be proud of the efforts as well as the outcomes.

That's why WE measure ourselves by outcomes, not activity.

CHAPTER 8

WE
CHALLENGE
EACH OTHER.
DIPLOMATICALLY.

" IF IT DOESN'T CHALLENGE YOU, IT DOESN'T CHANGE YOU.

"

—FRED DEVITO

WE 8

Several years ago, I had an employee named Drex Fitzwater who led a function called Strategic Workforce Planning. His team was responsible for the workforce management (forecasting, staffing, and scheduling) for an operation of roughly fifteen thousand people handling more than forty million phone calls a year. He led a large team doing a massively important job.

From early in our working relationship, Drex and I disagreed with each other—very diplomatically—about how to approach his function. I'd had Drex's job on a *much* smaller scale many years earlier in my career, and I was very familiar with that world. I've always thought workforce management was 90 percent science, 10 percent art; Drex thought it was the exact opposite, because even though he used software to do a fair amount of the work, he also regularly made subjective judgment calls by interpreting the data. For him, it wasn't just black-and-white.

However, from my estimation, Drex's insistence his job was 90 percent "art" meant he didn't lean on his team the way he could have. Instead, he was the funnel for all the info going in and out. He functioned almost as a gatekeeper. I also sensed he didn't effectively use all of the tools he had at his disposal—which would have made his team's job easier. As a result, a lot of his team's activity was reactive because his forecasts weren't as accurate as they should have been.

Drex and several members of his team had been together for many years. By most measuring sticks, Drex's team delivered a "good enough" product. So most of his former leaders didn't bother to push him or his team to do things much differently. They didn't completely understand how the team performed their work, so they never really challenged his approach. They hadn't seen other ways to do the job. I had.

Early in our tenure working together, Drex asked me, "How much of the job do you remember?"

I told him, "Just enough to be dangerous."

He chuckled as if to imply, "This guy is gonna be a pain in my ass."

He was right.

In every service operation I've ever led, I highly prioritized assessing the acumen of the workforce management team. Experience has taught me that not a lot matters if you can't forecast and staff with a high degree of accuracy—especially in an environment like a large call center operation. I look at it this way: every call that goes unanswered automatically receives a QA score of zero. You can't help if you don't answer the call.

And sure enough, after observing Drex and his team for a few months, I rocked the boat—a lot. My challenge to Drex was manifold, but the main theme was pushing him and his team to dig deeper into the years of historical data at their disposal. They needed to establish goals and thresholds for success criteria. They needed better reporting. And they needed to lean on technology, getting away from using Drex as the de facto oracle of forecasting. Finally, it all needed to be part of a massive improvement plan with clear goals for improvement and dates for achievement.

It's not my intention to tell this story via rose-colored glasses. It wasn't easy for me to be so openly critical about Drex's department. But it was *my job* to challenge. And allowing his team to continue operating with approaches I knew to be outdated and suboptimal is inauthentic leadership. I was incredibly difficult, yet diplomatic. I routinely challenged the way Drex's team operated. But I was never critical *of* Drex.

When I began to challenge basically everything he and his team were doing, Drex didn't flinch. He rose to the occasion in an impressive fashion. He confidently told me, "Whatever makes us better." And to his credit, he never let on that he was anything but fully invested in improving. He embarked on a massive transformation effort for his organization, taking it from barely average to above average and arguably best in class.

He hired an expert from the outside, implemented new procedures, developed new reporting, audited his team's skill base, and implemented required technology training for several members of his team. Within a few months, his forecast accuracy materially improved. His team was far less reactive, and they'd developed a new relationship with the data.

I love this story because Drex *heard* the challenge and made sure his team heard it too. Rather than be defensive of the organization he essentially built from the ground up, he passed on a sense of purpose and urgency to his team. Not only did he hear the challenge, but he responded in kind, challenging me. "Okay, Kyle," he said, "I need help getting us where you think we need to be. I need money for training, and I need to hire an expert who can bring us different perspectives." He was challenging me right back! We got him the needed resources, leading to dramatically improved results.

In a nutshell, folks, situations like this are exactly why WE *must* challenge each other. It simply must be part of the cultural DNA of your organization. When WE challenge each other, WE get better. If we're *not* challenging each other, by definition, we are not only accepting the status quo, we are promoting it.

Challenging each other simply must be part of the cultural DNA of the organization. When WE challenge each other, WE get better. If we're *not* challenging each other, by definition, we are not only accepting the status quo, we are promoting it.

"Challenge" Defined

But what does "WE challenge each other" really mean?

In Chapter 4, I covered the importance of taking action. As a reminder, taking action means recognizing an opportunity for improvement *and* making a move to address that opportunity—it's taking initiative.

WE 8 is the yang to WE 4's yin. While both WEs are required to drive a continuous improvement paradigm, they attack opportunities from different angles.

WE 4 requires you to make a move to address an identified opportunity within *your* domain. WE 8 requires you to push others on the team, including the leader, to constantly improve in *their* domain.

It doesn't mean you tell your coworker their operation sucks. It doesn't mean you point out all the deficiencies in their operation. And it doesn't mean you're allowed to spew criticism of others. Every challenge *must* be supported by data or experience. Challenges that begin with "I think" or "I feel" are subjective and usually come across as criticism, not genuine challenge. Challenge and criticism are not the same thing; challenge isn't even in the same ballpark as criticism. WE 8 does not provide license to criticize a decision you simply don't like.

However, it does allow for challenging in the spirit of improvement. And WE 8 gives everyone the same right to push the team to its highest and best potential. When you see ideas, processes, or plans that could be improved, regardless of title or who "owns" that domain, you are obliged to speak up—in a diplomatic, tactful way. When you or any member of the team identifies an opportunity to be better, in any way, the opportunity (a.k.a. challenge) must be discussed. There is absolutely no room for withholding fact-based opinions or relevant experience in a Culture of Excellence. I would much rather face an "I told you so" conversation than an "I knew that was going to fail" conversation.

This WE involves fostering evolution and continuous improvement among everyone on the team. It's not enough to rely on the boss to constantly raise the bar for each team member's performance. The bar setting must come from all.

In Chapter 2, I talked about Michael Jordan's approach to leading by example—he challenged his teammates at every opportunity—all in an effort to make them better and the team stronger.

Do you think the Bulls would have secured six NBA titles in eight years if Jordan worked only on his own game and simply assumed everyone else was doing the same? And do you think the same success would've come if Jordan had sat back and assumed the head coach would appropriately challenge everyone to improve? Of course, the answer to both questions is a resounding "no."

A team is a team, and the corporate setting should be no different. If you're a member of a team and you want the team to be the best, you must challenge those around you to be *their* best.

Issuing challenges must be engrained in the team's ethos. There are an infinite number of benefits that come from living this WE. But nothing worth having is easy—adopting this WE is *extremely* difficult—perhaps the toughest of any of the 10 WEs. Let's explore a few hurdles that can prevent this WE from being the rule rather than the exception.

Irony Alert: This One...Is Challenging

Challenge is a required ingredient for improvement. But I'm not naive; challenging others—your peers, your crew, and especially, your boss—can be a daunting prospect. Even more so when the legacy culture hasn't historically allowed for or encouraged it.

To examine why challenges are so elusive in most of Corporate America, let's first consider why people tend to avoid challenging each other in general. The primary reason is simple: most people prefer to avoid conflict whenever possible. Choosing to take the path of least resistance, not challenging others, is just easier. The more difficult path often results in conflict—and more work.

Sit Down—You're Rocking the Boat!

In the corporate world, there's a tendency to "get by." The prevailing approach is, "Easier is better and it keeps me employed; I'm not gonna rock the boat."

As a result, most bosses wait for a directive from "Leadership" before ever considering embarking on a higher standard or raising the bar. Why call attention to yourself or your team? Staying off "Leadership's" radar avoids conflict and reduces the likelihood of scrutiny and critical attention to themselves and their team.

Other times, it's "Management" who insists no one rock the boat. If something *looks* good enough, they don't want anyone else exposing areas of dysfunction or improvement opportunities. Here's an example: after a few months in my role at Maximus, I looked at our historical QA results and noticed we'd been achieving our goals nearly every single month, without fail, for years. My "too good to be true" alarms were chirping loudly. To learn more about why we were performing so well, I reached out to Brian Dye, the leader of our Training and Quality domain.

When I talked to Brian about this, I used the metaphor that the results were a bit like a test that everyone aces. No one should be breaking out the high fives in that scenario—the test is obviously too easy. If *everyone* succeeds, clearly the assessment is faulty. Likewise, if *everyone* fails—there's got to be a curve to show accurate results.

I challenged Brian to rewrite the entire program. Brian and his team spent months crafting a brand-new program, and we took it to the client. Their reaction was, "Uh, if you change this, our scores will go down. I'll get a bunch of pressure from my higher-ups about why our quality's slipping."

I can understand this reaction. Our client didn't want to draw attention with sagging results if it wasn't necessary. Rather than rock the boat and challenge his "higher-ups" to understand the benefit of continuously reassessing success criteria, it was easier to just leave it alone. Although our client didn't initially agree to our reimagined approach, we were ultimately able to find a new solution that still raised the bar for success without completely sinking our scores.

This comes with the territory of challenging one another. The first series of challenges may rock the boat to the point everyone is looking for a life vest. Once the first waves of resistance have calmed, a secondary challenge can still drive improvement—leaving you better off vs. never engaging in the first place.

Remember, challenges solve problems, but they usually do so by creating more work, changing the status quo, taking risks, trying new things, and other scary stuff. This tends to rock the boat in a big way.

It's Just Not My Place

How many times have you heard someone speak critically about something or someone else but then pause and add, "But who am I to judge?"

There is no room for this type of talk in a Culture of Excellence—where everyone has the same obligation to speak up (diplomatically) to share critical feedback.

I get it; many people don't feel comfortable critiquing others. We too often have a natural tendency to look the other way. Sometimes people don't feel entitled to voice a challenge; sometimes they don't feel it's their role to deliver critical feedback. But the truth is, it's everyone's role.

No One Told Me to, So I Didn't

Issuing a challenge to anyone, including the boss, requires mountains of courage. If looking critically at our processes and activities and making the effort to challenge them isn't on the "to-do" list, it doesn't get done.

My boss at Maximus didn't ask me to reinvent the quality wheel; I just thought it was the right thing to do. As far as he was concerned, they were fine—but he wasn't examining the data the same way I was.

If the boss isn't beating on the door, saying, "Raise the goal! Raise the success threshold!" people generally aren't going to create the extra work for themselves.

Challenging is doing the right thing, even if no one told you to do it.

Happy Happy? Joy Joy?

Some people snicker or even roll their eyes when I talk about how important it is to be happy at work. It's called "work," right? Not "play." However, many companies strive to make their employees happy, which is a great thing—until it isn't.

Making employees happy isn't a simple concept, and much of Corporate America takes the easy route—opting for superficial "unicorns-and-rainbows" over a deeper cultural transformation. They seek to eliminate conflict and promote warm fuzzies over transparency—a celebration of sterile mediocrity.

"Happy workers are more productive workers" makes a good bumper sticker. But is it an admirable rule to follow?

If that "happiness" exists because the environment is absent of challenges, the answer is an unequivocal "no." The appearance of happiness can mask unspoken tension and foster passive-aggressive behavior. However, an atmosphere of professional candor ensures a healthier work environment and eliminates the tendency for behind-the-back "feedback."

To achieve ambitious goals and find purpose in your work, there is no avoiding challenges. And by nature, challenges don't make most people happy. But it's the challenges, in both our personal and work lives, that allow us to grow and achieve. The growth doesn't always make people happy, but achievement certainly does.

No wonder "WE challenge each other" is the most difficult WE to deploy—there are good reasons to stay put, keep your head down, and your mouth closed. But lest you think that's the wise choice in the long run, let me make a case for the harder and better route of cultivating a culture where issuing challenges is standard operating procedure.

A (Cautionary) Tale of Two Fruit Companies

If you're reading this book on your phone or tablet, there's a strong possibility your device is made by a company named after a fruit: Apple. However, once upon a time, there was another company who sold a premium piece of handheld technology also named after a fruit: BlackBerry.

Originally known as Research in Motion (RIM), the Canadian company produced a slick lineup of handheld devices, the BlackBerry, which rose to prominence in the 1990s. With its physical QWERTY keyboard and proprietary software, BlackBerry was nothing short of revolutionary. The messenger tool, the device encryption, the user interface, the security were all best in class. BlackBerry products were light-years ahead of anything else, even into the early 2000s. They were the "smartphone" standard, especially for corporate users.

In those days I was a huge fan and owned several different BlackBerry devices. I was a devoted customer, vowing to never switch to another product, especially one without a physical keyboard. Who wants to type on a touch screen anyway? (Ahem.)

In the early 2000s, things started to get sticky. The consumer market wanted larger screens, and Android phones at the time began shifting to touchscreens for their smartphones. BlackBerry, however, kept its focus on the corporate market, leaving (the much larger) consumer market untapped. The company didn't challenge itself to evolve or expand its customer base to personal users; it simply focused on keeping its stranglehold on corporate usage—thinking never the twain shall meet. As more and more new Android models were debuting, BlackBerry products were updated but stayed mostly the same from year to year. The company bet everything on the software behind its devices without innovating their design or reconsidering their target user base.

Enter Apple.

Around the same time, Apple had a number of products that were thriving. The huge successes of the iMac, the iPod, and iTunes meant the company could have rested on its laurels, but no chance. Instead, it launched into something new in 2004, when it began developing what would become the iPhone.

After three years of development, the iPhone launched in 2007. Apple wasted no time updating and streamlining the product's design for not only the consumer market but also the corporate market. This too, was pure challenge in action: every year, the company would come up with a new version of the product, making it better, faster, sexier.

You know the rest of that story.

BlackBerry didn't challenge the status quo and lost its foothold in the smartphone market. The firm stopped making devices in 2017 and now focuses almost entirely on security software and services.

As recently as 2008, the two companies were very similar in terms of market capitalization—BlackBerry at $78 billion, Apple at $76 billion. However, innovation waits for no one. Today Apple is around $3 *trillion* while BlackBerry has atrophied to less than $4 billion.

And not coincidentally, Apple has built itself on an ethos of constant innovation: "challenge" is part of the company's DNA.

If you want your company, your team, and your professional reputation to be more than a cautionary tale, there's a lot to learn from this story. We need to continuously raise the threshold of success, be objective, embrace provocative thinking, challenge sacred cows, and encourage feedback from all.

Let's talk brass tacks.

The Foundation of a Challenge

Reconsider this idea that challenge is somehow a threat to peace and harmony. I'm not using "WE challenge each other" as an invitation to an argument or a duel. Instead, the act of challenging a person or some aspect of the status quo is a way to help that person or situation get *better*.

Challenging each other can be a slippery slope, but as the leader, it's your job to stop everyone from sliding down the mountain.

Diplomacy for the Win

It's no accident that WE 8 includes the word *diplomatically*. All challenges must be conducted in a civil way that conveys respect for all parties. The focus must always be on the issue or improvement opportunity, not the person involved—because a challenge is never personal. This is precisely why the challenge *must* be supported by data and/or experience. A challenge bolstered by data is hard to refute. And second to data is experience. For example, if we're in the planning phases of a new product release, and a member on the team has experience with this type of launch, gained from working in another firm, their challenge is one we better hear out. Certainly, context matters, but denying input from someone who has already done what we are trying to do is just plain arrogant.

If WE 8 is a drastic departure from your current environment, it might take several cycles before those on the receiving end of the challenge don't take it personally. (Stay tuned for WE 9, WE Embrace Challenge.) Until it becomes habit, leading with something like, "Hey, we challenge each other, right?" goes a long way in disarming the natural reaction to resist the challenge. This simple preemptive sentence removes any personal connection from the discussion. The quicker everyone is focused on the issue and relinquishes their sandbox ownership, the quicker we can focus on the opportunity and path to a better outcome.

CAN-DOr

A policy of objective transparency forces opportunities to the surface and allows you to lean on your team members' strengths and experiences when solving big problems. Even when it's uncomfortable (and it is, a lot), objective transparency creates an environment where it's safe to share fact-based opinions and information.

Embracing provocative thinking allows dialogue in a safe space to ask more questions: "Are we approaching XYZ in the right way? Is there another, better path?" These types of questions lead to better products for the client and improved outcomes for company and crew.

Whether solving a problem or creating a new policy or procedure, team members are obligated to ask fundamental questions of one another, like, "Why are we doing this? What if we didn't do this at all? Is this really the most efficient use of our resources? Who actually benefits from this?"

Candor promotes can-do.

Timing Is Key

This WE is not for the faint of heart and must be approached with caution—it takes time to build a culture where challenging one another is a common practice.

The best time to start incorporating challenge into daily life is when your company has declared it is actively seeking change. This change could come in the form of a new product launch, expansion of an existing product line, the win of a new client, or perhaps most ideal, an overt cultural transformation program.

And of course, being a new leader within the company provides a fantastic window to introduce WE 8 into the organization. But even in this scenario, timing matters—a lot. For example, I recognized the opportunities for improvement within Drex's team early in my role, but I deliberately waited until he and I had an open, trusting relationship before jumping into the deep end of the challenge pool. While entering an organization as a fresh set of eyes and objective voice provides a great opportunity to begin a WE-transformation, leaping straight to WE 8 risks alienating your team.

But what if your company isn't on the transformation train and you want to inspire a culture where challenging one another is the norm? Unfortunately, you can't just roll into your next staff meeting and declare, "This is how we do things now: *WE CHALLENGE*," offer some fist bumps, and leave. They'll think you're a naive, out of touch asshole who just read a new leadership book. Instead, be deliberate about *when* you start to push your company's culture in this direction.

There is a reason this WE comes late in the list of ten. If the first WE was *WE Challenge Each Other,* the culture would be intolerable and lead to anarchy. No one feels comfortable issuing challenges in a culture that doesn't pride itself on doing the right thing, where every member of the team is expected to lead by example, and especially where people aren't free to make (and own) mistakes because they know they will be picked up. The first seven WEs must be adopted *and* lived before venturing into WE 8.

When you are "there," don't make any grand proclamations or stump speeches. Simply tell your team you have a new (or renewed, depending on your relationship with your team) interest in giving a voice to anyone who has data or experience that could help solve a problem or make us better in any sense. Don't expect an avalanche of folks challenging one another—the crew first needs to see how you respond to challenges (many times) before they jump on board. Don't beat around the bush using corporate speak. Tell them you expect to be challenged and replay the message over and over, even reminding them when you're making a process or policy decision—seek to be challenged.

You may not be able to be quite as aggressive with challenging your leader or even your peers—more on this later in the chapter—but you can cultivate a safe space for challenges within your own team. From there, you'll begin to recognize a growing willingness to push for change in other areas of your company.

Even within a culture that's fully embraced WE 8, it's still important to remember time and place matter—especially when challenging the boss. Don't do it in a group setting. This has the potential to go badly and you stand to alienate the other person. For example, you wouldn't want to issue a challenge during a town hall—calling out a coworker in front of an audience. Using a public venue to issue a challenge has the appearance of grandstanding and comes across like a personal attack.

Outcomes Aren't Personal

A surefire way to *delay* the adoption of this WE is to allow challenges that are subjective or even personal. This is a fast path to dysfunction. There is only one way to guarantee your challenge is not taken personally: tie it directly to an outcome. When I challenge you on an outcome that is objectively underperforming, it's not personal because the outcome is the focus, not your inability to hit that outcome.

Here's a good example. Every company has its own approach to the budgeting process. At a minimum, there is an annual effort to forecast for the following year. But most companies refine at least quarterly, if not monthly. Anyone who has ever been responsible for a P&L or owned operating expenses has participated in this song and dance: "corporate" provides a target you and your teams must hit. And more often than not, the number given requires a tightening of the belt, so to speak, in one or more areas of spending. This, of course, has the potential of cutting where you couldn't afford to cut, simply for the sake of hitting a number, rather than budgeting what's actually needed for the team to achieve its goals. Even tougher for the crew, some functional areas might need to cut a bigger percentage than their peers. This never goes well and leaves the unlucky leader feeling as if the cut is personal.

I've been involved in this process too many times to count. No surprise, when I've had to ask one or more of my direct reports to cut their team/function's budget, the response isn't usually gratitude. My approach: rather than individually working with *several* of my leaders to determine the size of their respective "haircut," I bring all my directs into a room and issue *one* challenge—collectively, we have a target to hit—so *collectively*, we make the decisions for places to cut. Issuing a challenge with a targeted outcome—in this case, a macro budget reduction—removes the chance of my challenge being perceived as personal.

Sidenote: this approach also promotes sharing of information among peers, and much more importantly, it aligns them on one common goal that can only be accomplished with teamwork and cooperation.

Using outcomes makes the situation black-and-white because it's always leading back to something tangible and quantifiable.

Consistently Raise the Threshold for Success

Hitting a goal one time should be the first step in a trend. Once a trend becomes habit and is routinely achieved, it's time to consider raising the bar for success. Success yesterday should not automatically mean success tomorrow.

When you've got a metric and your team is consistently achieving that target, don't continue to do high fives every month. Instead, revisit the metric. Evaluate whether it should be updated or if it's still the right threshold of success. If you're still referencing the same goals now as you were three years ago, I'm sorry to tell you, you're not raising the bar and aren't improving.

Consumer expectations aren't the same as three years ago; therefore, your own expectations for success need to continually rise as well.

Send Those Sacred Cows Out to Pasture

The absolute worst thing anyone can ever say to me is, "We've always done it this way." This cop-out statement embodies complacency and models an embrace of the status quo. All I can ever say in response is, "Well, why?" Most of the time, people reiterate the old chestnut in different ways: "Because that's the way it's always been done."

If you don't look to innovate your processes, expect the same results. Just don't expect improvement. That's why areas "that have always been done this way"—those sacred cows—are a prime target for challenges. We must look to improve and grow beyond the status quo. A culture in which people challenge each other in the ways I've just listed will be one that is constantly innovating, prioritizing excellence, and creating a safe space for dialogue.

Ask and Be Open to "Dumb" Questions

There really are no dumb questions. This may seem cliché to some, but it's absolutely true in a Culture of Excellence. Every question has value, especially if it's one people think they *shouldn't* ask. An environment in which challenges are commonplace encourages all questions and makes certain no one feels they'll be chastised for asking them—especially questions related to those sacred cows. Asking questions is the foundation for a new challenge.

For instance, early in my time at CVS, I was tasked with modernizing the organization's self-service capabilities, including the interactive voice response (IVR) platform for our Specialty Pharmacy business. You already know (and probably dislike) these touchtone systems: they're the recorded menus you hear when you call a large company that tell you to, "Press one for _____." Ostensibly, no one had explored creating a better caller experience in Specialty, so I issued a clear challenge to the VP of that area: make it easier to use—make it user-friendly and conversational.

At the time, before the caller was even prompted to enter a single digit, our IVR led off with a laundry list of facts about the local store the caller was attempting to reach, including the address and phone number.

This felt unnecessary and clunky, so I asked, "Why do we include all that?"

The team said, "Well, we have to. It's a compliance thing. We *must* provide the physical address and read back the store's phone number." Their quick reaction and tone made their thoughts clear: the new guy looked like, well, the new guy—what a dumb question!

"Okay," I said. "Can somebody show me that? I'd like somebody to show me the language from the compliance regulations that says we have to do this."

At the time, I realized that there was a good chance I was going to come out of this particular challenge looking like an ignorant asshole, but I just couldn't shake the feeling that something wasn't right.

Turns out, no one within our legal or compliance teams could find a shred of evidence that this greeting was *required*. The language didn't exist. We were about to make a typically dreadful experience no better by bothering the caller with information they didn't need to know—like the phone number they had *just* dialed— because someone thought that was required.

I'm sharing this story not because I was right, but because questioning everything really does mean asking questions about every damn thing you can. In this case, I had to challenge to verify their sacred cow assumption—which prompted the team to find out what the regulations actually said. Or in this case, didn't say. The end result was an improved, less clunky caller experience.

But pretend such a compliance requirement really did exist. That would have been okay too. My "dumb question" was an effort to improve my customers' experience—and that's a dumb question worth asking.

The moral here: don't be afraid to ask a question just because you're afraid to look bad. And don't underestimate the example you're setting when you ask "dumb" questions. You're establishing a safe space for inquisitive minds to flourish.

Challenges in All Directions

Picture this scenario in a company that has yet to embrace WE 8: in your boss's staff meeting, you run through your update; the six other people at the table who aren't your boss potentially don't give a shit and may not even be listening. Why should they? The only person in the room who's "allowed" to challenge the information you've given is the boss. This entire scenario is wildly inefficient. Why give reports to the whole team if only one person's opinion matters?

Challenging members of the team comes with the territory for leaders. But challenges shouldn't *only* come from the leader. To foster a challenge-rich environment, peers must challenge peers, and—wait for it—subordinates should be encouraged to challenge their leaders.

Peer to Peer

Peer-to-peer challenges are an incredibly important ingredient for building a Culture of Excellence—because they are born from one's motivation to see another, and the team, succeed.

It's especially critical to give diplomatic feedback to people who are on your same team. Every member of a high-performing team pulls their own weight. When one team member doesn't, their peers must be comfortable to challenge them directly. This approach creates a shared sense of responsibility for the team's success, and in this kind of environment, it's more difficult for one team member to be the slacker outlier. The ultimate goal of WE 8 is to provide the person responsible for executing—in this scenario, your peer—with alternate perspectives, data, and experiences in order to help them improve.

> Peer-to-peer challenges are an incredibly important ingredient for building a Culture of Excellence—because they are born from one's motivation to see another, and the team, succeed.

You're not challenging your peer to live up to *your* standard. You're pushing them to live up to *the team's* standard. In fact, your *opinion* that a teammate is slacking doesn't matter at all. You have to quantify your challenge. Without data and objective transparency, you're just bitching.

When done properly, challenges are a way to support each other—not to tear each other down.

I recognize some people don't feel comfortable with confrontation or don't want to hurt others' feelings by pointing out problems with their work—but you have an obligation here. If you're one of five direct reports, and you and three others are busting your asses to make the team successful, while the fifth is not delivering work that's up to par, it's healthier (in the long run) to issue the challenge. Do it diplomatically, but *do it*—at least once. It isn't your job to coach or counsel your teammate; leave that to your leader.

The alternative: you end up stewing in your observations, leading to other critical opinions, and resentment ensues. This benefits no one. You'll become bitter and eventually disengage. Work becomes a chore rather than an environment where you feel you can make a difference.

In the end, you have to focus less on what you can do individually, and more on what *WE* can do as a team. If you want your team or company to be the best—or even just better—challenges must be an everyday activity.

Even as the leader of a team, you likely have peers. It's also good for your directs to see you challenging them. This not only normalizes and fosters peer-to-peer challenges within your team; it also opens the door for the team to challenge you.

Subordinate to Leader

In many environments, challenging a peer may come easily, but challenging a leader is tough to imagine and tougher to execute.

But remember, the ultimate goal of WE 8 is to provide the decision maker—in this scenario, the leader—with alternate perspectives, data, and experiences so they can land on the optimal (and improved) solution. Failure to do so devolves the team into a complacent, passive, head nodding, apathetic environment.

> The ultimate goal of WE 8 is to provide the decision maker—in this scenario, the leader—with alternate perspectives, data, and experiences so they can land on the optimal (and improved) solution.

With that said though, the desire to voice a challenge to your boss should be balanced with the practical context of the boss's leadership style and the level of authenticity you've observed to date. If your leader is on board, driving (or helping to drive) a WE-oriented paradigm, a challenge aimed their direction *should* be well received.

As always, especially with the boss, approach the situation diplomatically. Consider saying something like, "Are you open to another angle? If so, I think I have some information you might want to consider." Diplomatic? Yes. Unassuming? You bet. Respectful of the chain of command? Absolutely (and always). How you frame the challenge is important. Approaching the challenge in a way that comes across like a question rather than a statement of fact can yield a great response. I've had bosses who are receptive to these diplomatic challenges. Bosses like this *do* exist, even in a *typical* corporate culture.

However, I've also had bosses who say, "I'm not open to hearing other opinions on this." If this sounds like your boss, just move on. Focus your energies instead on transforming the culture within your team and among your peers. The boss's inability to embrace challenges should not dictate your desire to promote WE 8 within your own team.

Subordinates can and should deliver challenges to their leaders, but these challenges land most effectively when the leader is open to suggestions, the case is presented with evidence and diplomacy, and there's an emphasis on improved team outcomes.

The "WE Challenge Each Other" Challenge

Every time I've delivered a Begin With WE address, either as a leader or executive coach, I'm either asked which of the 10 WEs is my "favorite" and/or which is the "toughest."

My answer is the same for both questions—WE 8: WE Challenge Each Other. Ironically, it's my favorite *because it is* the toughest for most cultures to embrace. But when you get there, the impact is so profoundly rewarding. Never settling for "good enough" is the most important factor for building a Culture of Excellence. If everyone is okay with "good enough," there is no need for challenges and no need for courageous leadership. On the contrary, the number one tool to break through the mediocrity of "good enough" is a well-thought-out challenge that opens eyes and minds to higher standards.

Besides, how unfulfilling is "good enough"? Where is the fun in just checking proverbial boxes and delivering the same shit over and over? Pushing mediocre boundaries, questioning sacred cows, and challenging others to excel, results in a better product and stronger teams—both of which will garner attention from the rest of your organization—and your clients.

I can say from experience, being part of a team that constantly pushes for improvement is ridiculously fun *and* rewarding. Yes, fun! But don't be fooled, sometimes we get frustrated and even mad because there are setbacks. No matter how tight the team, challenges are tough and can make anyone uncomfortable. But the discomfort wanes as WE 8 becomes the standard.

Remember, you're an expedition leader helping your team navigate an upward climb. When the crew makes real progress and reaches an important base camp on the way to the peak of the mountain, it's fantastic to just stop and look back at the progress made. Remembering how difficult it was on the way up provides important perspective for appreciating where we are now.

> Remembering how difficult it was on the way up provides important perspective for appreciating where we are now.

That perspective allows you, the expedition leader, to take a deep breath and relax for a moment—and then say, "Well, we've still got to climb higher; let's get back at it."

I love it. I can't get enough.

Think back to the challenges I presented to Drex. Initially, he and I weren't aligned on his team's mission, and we hadn't yet bonded in an authentic way. And although my challenges weren't personal, I knew his mettle would be tested. Many years have passed, and I was curious to see if our efforts from those days had a lasting impact on him and his team. In a recent email to me, Drex was kind enough to document his thoughts on how the 10 WEs shaped his leadership and benefited him and his team. I'd like to share that with you:

> Since embracing the 10 WEs, a true transformational shift has occurred, not only in my professional life with the way I operate and manage, but with how I go about my personal life too. Professionally, they have brought teams closer, increased our drive for continuous improvement, and created an environment of transparency and honesty. People now foster an environment of constant change, can easily reflect on accomplishments, and

have stronger relationships within the organization. I've never seen a team grow so passionate and dedicated. Personally, I've learned to challenge myself, reflect on the things I've done, and continually tell myself to do the right thing.

Drex's words illustrate the other important side of the "continuous improvement coin"—the personal and professional growth that comes when WE *embrace* the challenge. And we do so not because it's easy, but because it's the right thing to do and we want to be better.

As we move into WE 9—the penultimate WE—I'd like to challenge you to sit completely still for a moment and look back at how far we've come together. I'm glad you're still with me.

Deep breath in, deep breath out.

Now let's get back to it.

CHAPTER 9

WE
EMBRACE
CHALLENGE.

"
IF YOU LIVE IN ONE FOR TOO LONG, IT BECOMES YOUR NORM. GET COMFORTABLE BEING UNCOMFORTABLE.
"

—DAVID GOGGINS, ON COMFORT ZONES

WE 9

About fifteen years ago, I found myself forced to embrace challenge. I remember it like it was yesterday.

At the time, I was a younger guy, leading a workforce of several thousand employees for a multibillion-dollar healthcare company. I spent half a dozen years there, working inside one of the most intense and hard-charging cultures with which I've ever been associated. The company's CEO was an aggressive, thirty-something-year-old guy with incredibly high expectations, and he fostered a company culture that wasn't for the meek.

A top executive, the Chief Medical Officer, was an ornery guy named Ace Hodgin. Ace was probably in his mid- to late sixties at the time and was widely known for being cantankerous in most settings. He didn't seem to mind offending people or hurting feelings. If he thought your results sucked, he would say, "Your results suck!"

My first experience being on the receiving end of Ace's challenging ways was during a monthly operations review meeting. Every month, leaders came together to share their team's results and discuss improvement efforts. When we made it to my portion of the agenda, I presented like I did most months, and I remember feeling it was going fairly well. However, there was a particular performance metric that wasn't where it needed to be for the second month in a row. I acknowledged it but quickly followed with assurance that my team was all over it and noted the metric was trending in the right direction. Ace took exception. As he was known to do, he challenged the *pace* of our improvement.

My response can only be described as annoyed and defensive. He pushed; I dug in. He pushed more; I dug in more. The exchange started to make others uncomfortable, even awkward—the room was full of silent people looking down at their BlackBerries, wishing they were somewhere else (me included).

Eventually, Ace moved on, and that was that—or so I thought. When I left the meeting, I wasn't pissed off or worked up; my only thought was, "That's just Ace."

Later the same day, I was summoned to the principal's office. Ace's assistant got me on the phone: "Hey, Ace wants to see you. Can you stop by?"

I'd worked with Ace for some time, but I'd never been asked to "stop by." Ace's office was in a different building across campus, and I still remember that walk feeling like it lasted an eternity. Dreading what was in store, I tapped on his door, white-knuckled and ready for my medicine—whatever that might be.

However, I was in for a surprise.

With a tone as warm and inviting as a grandfather, Ace welcomed me in and said, "Kyle, really happy you could come see me. I don't know you that well. Tell me about your background."

I'll never forget the shock of that moment. Ace was so charming— hell, even likable—a side of him I had never come close to seeing. We talked for about twenty minutes, and I couldn't help but think of Jekyll and Hyde. His demeanor was *the polar opposite* of what I'd dealt with just hours earlier.

Eventually, Ace artfully took the conversation back to that morning's meeting. "Here comes the lambasting," I thought.

"In today's meeting, you were pretty damn defensive about your results," Ace said.

I couldn't tell if he was being sarcastic, if he was baiting me, or if he was just sharing a general observation.

"No shit," I thought. But out loud, I said, "Yeah, I was defensive. Sure. You challenged the results that my team has been delivering, and I'm proud of the progress we've made. Maybe they're not quite where we need them to be, but that trajectory is what we want."

It quickly became obvious; Ace was more focused on *me* and not the results.

He gave me a long look, and with a slight grin, he said, "You're taking this personally."

"Well, yeah. I am," I said. "I've been working incredibly hard to get us back on track, Ace. So, yes, I *do* take this stuff very personally."

Ace leaned in my direction and quietly offered a one-word reply: "Don't."

"What do you mean, 'don't'?"

"The sooner you learn to take none of this personally, the better you will be throughout your entire career," he said. "When you take it personally, you lose your objectivity, and your judgment becomes cloudy."

This single conversation with Ace changed how I approach my work and instilled the value of unemotionally focusing on outcomes, in pursuit of achieving goals. Ace was right: the more *emotionally* invested you are in your team's performance, the less clearly you see what's really happening. Particularly when managing metrics, the leader's ability to think objectively is clouded when operating from a place of emotion rather than logic and fact. Rather than focusing on *doing* what's right, an emotionally defensive leader merely focuses on *being* right.

> The more *emotionally* invested you are in your team's performance, the less clearly you see what's really happening.

Although I wouldn't have expressed it the same way back then, the hindsight is clear. It was that conversation with Ace where I learned WE must embrace challenge.

The (Need for) Struggle Is Real

Yes—I dedicated an entire chapter to the importance of challenges. But when building a Culture of Excellence, issuing challenges is only half of the equation. Without an *embrace* of those challenges, that excellence never arrives.

So why is WE Embrace Challenge significant enough to be its own WE? The answer is simple: nearly everything is achieved via a challenge.

In 1962, during a speech where he shared an audacious challenge of landing a man on the moon, President Kennedy proclaimed, "We choose to go to the moon in this decade, and do other things, not because they are easy, but because they are hard." Kennedy was right—nothing worth having is easy.

This ideal also applies to business and leadership but can be a hard notion for many to accept. Because for most, a challenge in the workplace elicits an all-too-common response of, "That *can't be* done!" The more productive response is to ask, "*Why can't* it be done?"

Embracing the challenge and plotting the response is a requirement for growth. Think of this in fitness terms: if you want bigger, stronger muscles, you've got to challenge the muscles with weights or other forms of resistance. The resistance literally tears the fibers in your muscles, forcing them to grow back bigger and stronger.

You've got to endure a certain amount of pain and discomfort before breaking through, stronger on the other side. The only way to get to the other side is by *embracing* the challenge, not running from it. In fact, growing stronger from challenges is a fundamental component of the human existence. Our immune system is the perfect example—it *must* have threats and challenges like bacteria and viruses to grow stronger and ultimately fend off those same threats.

Breakups, divorces, losing a loved one—all represent challenges most of us have experienced, or will experience, at one point or another. It's only natural that we associate most challenges with negativity. Challenges in the workplace are no different—they can feel deeply uncomfortable and even personal, like my experience with Ace.

That challenge-averse mentality has become a plague inside Corporate America—where the safety that comes from mediocrity outweighs the benefit of a challenging breakthrough.

To Give, You Must Receive

The last chapter was dedicated to the importance of issuing challenges to your team, your peers, and your leader. To authentically challenge others in the organization, you must be prepared to receive them as well.

To model and foster an environment where everyone pushes everyone else to innovate and excel, leaders must *embrace* each challenge. Whether internally generated (from the boss, a peer, or a team member) or externally born (environmental, economic, or a competitive threat), the challenge must be recognized and embraced—that is, if we want to grow, improve, and win.

This is why WE 9 gets its own chapter. Let's talk about the importance of instilling a "WE embrace challenge" paradigm.

What Kind of "Embrace" Are We Talking About?

I'm a big hugger. I always have been. A heartfelt embrace is a great way of communicating care for another. But I also recognize hugging may not be for everyone. If you fall into this category, sorry to say, you don't get a free pass on WE 9. A literal embrace is not what I'm talking about.

The word *embrace* also means "an act of accepting or supporting something willingly or enthusiastically"—and that's the kind of embrace you'll need to keep in mind during this WE.

> Embrace is an act of accepting or supporting something willingly or enthusiastically—and that's the kind of embrace you'll need to keep in mind during this WE.

Willingly and *enthusiastically* might be the most powerful words in the definition. You can accept and support challenge in all kinds of ways, but doing it consciously and with enthusiasm is what drives growth.

In the years since that oddly inspiring meeting with Ace, I've come to deliver and accept challenges readily—even daily. Yes, even willingly and enthusiastically. I certainly didn't start out that way; I had to learn to embrace challenge by overcoming my own hangups. After getting over myself and setting ego aside, I realized just how much could be gained by embracing challenge as a rule.

The process for reacting to a challenge must involve gaining an ability to figuratively rise above yourself and the person who's issuing the challenge, to observe from a distance.

Ideally, especially in a WE-oriented culture, the challenges hurled your way won't be personal. But even if they are, you aren't obliged to *embrace* them personally. Truly embracing the challenge means removing your personal bias, putting your subjectivity aside, and assuming positive intent: "Okay, if this person is approaching me from a place of good intention and real experience, then I should hear them out."

*Sidenote: ironically, dealing with challenges that **aren't** the result of positive intent represents a challenge in and of itself. However, challenges of this nature must likewise be embraced.*

A person's embrace of a challenge isn't so much an "either/or" decision, but falls on a spectrum we'll call the "Embrace-O-Meter." On one end, there's obstinance—a total resistance to challenge. On the other, there's willing and enthusiastic embrace. Leaders must find ways to get (and keep) their people from one end of the spectrum to the other. You're human, and your team is made up of humans. So just remember, this is an ongoing process requiring constant focus.

OPEN-MINDED　　　WILLING

OBSTINATE　　　ENTHUSIASTIC

Moving the needle on the Embrace-O-Meter *can* happen. I'm living proof! Depending on where you start, moving from one end of that spectrum to the other can take years—and that's okay. It's also okay if that evolution takes place dramatically—like, after one conversation from someone you really respect. What matters is that you're regularly checking where your team's attitudes fall on the Embrace-O-Meter, choosing to move your culture in the right direction: toward growth, toward authenticity, toward excellence.

The Benefits of Embracing Challenge

In the last chapter, I talked about one of my proudest career achievements. I'd like to go a little deeper into that story because it highlights some unexpected benefits associated with taking on a big challenge.

It was 2014 and I was working for Optum. I'd been asked to lead the bailout of several state-based health insurance exchanges. These were states that had rejected the federal version of the Affordable Care Act, opting to launch a state-run marketplace instead—and flopped. My team was charged with "smoke-jumping" in to rescue those faltering states, and thankfully, we were able to deliver outcomes that benefited everyone. I worked with a number of governors and their cabinet officials to develop rescue plans to avail healthcare to hundreds of thousands of people in these states. This six-month window of time was without question, the hardest I've ever worked. It was a wild experience, and I never could have predicted the far-reaching benefits that were realized from embracing this challenge. The whole experience was good for the company, the customer, and my crew.

The company: My team's efforts generated close to $40 million in unplanned revenue that year. Word got out that Optum was playing a role in these states' "bailouts"; stock-market analysts picked up on that, along with the cash we were bringing in. The company's revenue, public profile, and reputation all benefited. You can't buy that kind of press—but you can earn it by embracing challenge.

The customer: Technically, in each of these engagements, the state we supported was our customer. And our state customers benefited tremendously. But more important was the impact we had on so many of these states' citizens. Government-sponsored healthcare isn't just big business; it's a necessary service that brings affordable insurance to millions of people—but only if they can get it. In one state, there was an application backlog that had ballooned to nearly seventy-five thousand people prior to my team and me hitting the ground. These were men and women (and their children) who needed coverage but were unable to get it because the state failed to launch a functioning enrollment system. If it weren't for the efforts of so many at Optum, there is no way to know how much longer they would have been without healthcare.

The crew: Many members of my team have catapulted to impressive positions as a result of their embrace of this challenge as well. John Kettering, who I mentioned in Chapter 2, assumed my role when I departed for Maximus and has since taken on progressively bigger roles within Optum. Another team member moved on to become the Global Head of Assessment technology at Amazon. A third member of my team was ultimately propelled to the position of COO at an Optum subsidiary.

These are just a few examples of members of the crew who recognized an opportunity to have a big impact, embraced the challenge, and personally benefited from their efforts. But they weren't alone.

Embracing the challenge was good for me as well. Because I played a leading role in Optum's efforts—one that was noticed by the press and other companies in the government sector—doors opened for me too. I'm certain I would've never been given the opportunity to join Maximus, a government contractor, if I hadn't been front and center of this effort. The size, scale, and complexity of my role at Maximus, in turn, led to my position at CVS.

You see, when you embrace a challenge, you have an opportunity to drive change that has a lasting impact. But to be clear, it's not just *embracing* the challenge that counts; you must deliver as well. Overcoming the obstacles that come with big problems enables growth. I talked before about building up a muscle—the strain of physical exercise creates small tears in the muscle; as the muscle repairs itself, it becomes stronger, enabling the growth. When you take risks and put in the work to meet a challenge, that effort enables growth on many levels.

Because growth and continuous improvement are inextricably linked, in order to continue to grow, you have to keep pushing yourself—continually improving—every day.

Put simply: the absence of challenge is the enemy of growth.

I'm Ready to Embrace Challenge! (But How?)

While every challenge comes with its own variables to consider, there are some tried-and-true strategies for embracing both internal and external opportunities. Since we cannot predict the emergence of external challenges and since internal challenges don't come with guided instructions, your ability to turn a challenge into growth starts with your choice to embrace it as such.

Keep an Open Mind

The first real step to embracing challenge is keeping an open mind. No matter how much you think you know about a topic, you have blind spots. The more quickly you acknowledge you don't know something, the closer you are to genuine open-mindedness. You cannot appreciate what you cannot see.

But for argument's sake, let's say you *do* know everything about a particular subject. Is there harm to being open-minded enough to consider alternative information? No. What's the worst thing that can happen? Nothing. When you keep an open mind while being challenged, there are only two possible outcomes: first, you learn something. Or second, the person issuing the challenge learns something.

Simply put:

- Know what you know: without arrogance or ego, it's your obligation to teach others who are interested to learn from you.
- Know (and admit) what you don't know: without shame or self-consciousness, ask others to help you bridge your knowledge gap.

The *me*-oriented leader sits alone in a silo and refuses all help, saying, "I've got this. I know this. I've been here. I've done this well in the past." Denying yourself the option of being vulnerable because of arrogance limits your growth opportunities. The boss who *knows everything* perpetuates the Leadership Gap and alienates themselves from the team. You're not going to get better, and neither is your team.

Even worse is the boss who pretends to know everything. This just in: your team is already well aware of your weaknesses and knowledge gaps. Most likely, they're bumping into them every day. Pretending to possess knowledge that you don't will solidify you as an inauthentic leader, losing you the respect of your team.

You must be self-aware enough to understand your limitations as a solo act. Remember, your title doesn't grant you exclusive access to all the best and brightest ideas. Being a Manager, a Director, an executive, etc., isn't a ticket to omniscience, so don't let your ego take over. Instead, keep an open mind that an alternative perspective could be enlightening—shedding light on your blind spots.

Don't...

It's difficult to emotionally detach when someone challenges you—especially if you care deeply about what you do. We feel a sense of satisfaction when we feel we've done a job well, and a challenge can disrupt that sense of satisfaction. It can feel as if you've exposed a weakness or a flaw; you may feel that the value of your work has been undermined or that the value you place in yourself has been minimized. I get it. You put a lot of effort and time into your work. It's easy to receive a challenge as criticism and take it personally.

But as Ace so eloquently taught me, "Don't."

When he challenged me, I had a hard time separating myself and my own value from the work my team was delivering; I took it personally initially. In some ways, it's admirable to have that kind of responsibility and passion. However, when that passion gets in the way of the growth and continuous improvement that we've already determined is a crucial part of success, it's a problem.

No Credit, No Blame

In a WE-oriented culture, we put aside feelings of blame and who deserves credit. Concern about either only clouds the continuous improvement process. Focusing on blame drives feelings of inadequacy, hampering your ability to courageously lead. Similarly, focusing on credit inflates your sense of value, creating a divide between yourself and your team.

This is part of ridding the corporate environment of the me-focus—making way for the WE culture.

Assume You're Wrong

Assuming you have all the answers is essentially the Incumbent's Curse on a personal level. In Chapter 4, I covered the Incumbent's Curse at the macro level—where companies are so enamored with their success, they fail to see the next innovation or radically new opportunity. If you allow it, the same curse can exist for you. In other words, it's important to be aware that you are likely biased to a specific solution—especially if you created the solution. Assuming you're wrong allows you to objectively see the innovation or superior solution that may come with a challenge.

Know What I Mean

When you are on the receiving end of a challenge, it's critical to make sure you thoroughly understand the scenario before you react. If challenges aren't commonplace in your environment, a challenge can be uncomfortable and trigger an automatic physiological fight-or-flight reaction, making it impossible to accurately *hear* what the other person is saying.

This of course, is a problem that can be overcome. In order to really embrace the challenge, you must "press pause" and take the time to recognize what's been presented. So many people jump right to "solution mode" without ever fully grasping the problem. You simply cannot effectively address the issue until you fully understand the nuances of the challenge and recognize a potential opportunity for growth through solving it.

When solving a problem, there are usually multiple ways to go about it. The challenge isn't about *how* to solve the problem, per se, but in fully understanding *what* is being challenged, in all its complexity.

'Tis the Reason(ing)

When discussing a challenge, pay less attention to people's opinions and more attention to the *reasoning* that led them to deliver their challenge in the first place. Again, assume they're considering something you haven't. Different perspectives bring different conclusions. Certainly, at times, you will face challenges that have a shaky foundation, when the data or experiences being touted are less than relevant. Try to follow the thought process they used to generate the challenge, and don't get hung up on *how* it was presented.

Think of this like math homework. Your teacher always wanted you to "show your work," right? The teacher needed to see *how* you got the answer. Showing your work wasn't only to verify you actually did the work. If you got the question wrong, it also helped the teacher identify where in the process you erred.

This approach can be helpful in understanding the root of someone's challenge. Prompt your team member to "show their work." Understanding *how* their process led them to issue the challenge uncovers different perspectives and related conclusions that you may have never considered.

Lead the Embrace

To effectively drive a culture to be comfortable with and grow from embracing challenge, the leader must pave the way. The way you receive challenges sets the example for your team to follow.

Regardless of whether the challenge is internal or external, the team takes its cue from you.

If the challenge was born from an external event, be genuine with your team, recognize the situation without sugarcoating, and remind them of the strength that comes from your collective response. There is goodwill to be gained from always reminding the team, "We are in this together."

If the challenge came from a member of the team, a peer, or even "Management," the team will keenly watch (and replicate) your embrace of the challenge or lack thereof.

In either scenario, don't run from the adversity. Rather, acknowledge its existence and lean in to one another to overcome and grow.

Willingly and enthusiastically embracing challenge is a fundamental requirement for continuous improvement and growth. Ace Hodgin knew the importance of taking a challenge at face value, and I'm better for the coaching he offered.

Very few people are comfortable with challenge initially. And you may *never* get yourself or every member of the crew all the way to the "willing and enthusiastic" end of the Embrace-O-Meter. However, when you methodically and continuously nudge everyone over to that side of the spectrum, embracing challenge becomes part of the culture.

Setting ego aside and genuinely embracing challenges may feel impossible at first. It may even kick your ass for a while. Challenges that are connected to something you've created or for which you are responsible will be the toughest to embrace. But these are the type of challenges that, when embraced, result in the most significant growth, both personally and in the workplace. Every bit of effort you dedicate toward growth is making you—and as a result, your team—stronger. Consciously push past your resistance, take it on, grow, and improve.

CHAPTER 10

WE
OBSESS
OVER DETAILS.
DETAILS MATTER.
A LOT.

"

THE DETAILS ARE NOT THE DETAILS. THEY MAKE THE PRODUCT.

"

—CHARLES EAMES

WE 10

Let's say you want to build a wall that requires one thousand beautiful red bricks. Preparing for the build day, you've hired a reputable bricklayer and had the bricks delivered to the jobsite.

For the wall to be perfectly level, *every brick* must be perfectly level—especially the bricks at the base. Allowing for a very small margin of error, the amount and application of mortar must be consistent from left to right and top to bottom. If the bricklayer is obsessed with these details, the end product is a perfectly true wall—every layer of brick and every ounce of mortar is consistent, leaving a wall that is level from end to end.

Now imagine what happens if the bricklayer uses a little too much mortar at just *one* joint. This seemingly insignificant detail causes the next brick laid to be slightly askew. With one brick applied, the mistake might even be too small to notice. Mathematically, we're only talking about one of one thousand bricks or **one-tenth of one percent** being "off."

However, by the time the bricklayer has added several more layers on top of the lopsided brick at the bottom, the problem is much more pronounced. Having just one brick off by a fraction at the base sets off a chain reaction of increasingly uneven bricks. The end result: a brick wall that bows upward and is noticeably uneven at the top.

Everything has been compromised by one missed detail.

The bricks in a wall are very much like the details needed to execute in most scenarios in business. Missing one "minor" detail in the beginning can seem trivial and inconsequential—but that minor detail can lead to significant ramifications as time goes on.

Several years ago at Optum, my team and I were at a client's office to deliver a pitch to add additional business to our portfolio. This was a client who had a reputation of being notoriously difficult and confrontational. My team and I knew we needed to bring our A Game to the meeting.

A few slides into the meeting, I thought it was going very well—until suddenly it wasn't. While covering a slide early in the presentation, a member of my team, Brian, was abruptly interrupted by our client. She'd spotted a number that didn't pass her sniff test.

Unassumingly, she asked, "Are you sure that number is right?"

Brian didn't hesitate. He confidently said, "It's right. We double- and triple-checked these numbers."

He tried to move along, but she was fixated on this one number—in a presentation of more than twenty pages. Growing annoyed, she pressed him to check it, and Brian pushed back a second time, diplomatically. This response further irritated her—which, to be fair, was easy to do.

Our client shook her head and mumbled something under her breath. Not to be deterred, and confident in our numbers, my team and I continued through the presentation, flipping from one page to the next. Our client, however, never turned the page and never asked another question. She unplugged.

The meeting ended with no smiles and an awkward, "I'll get back to you" from our client. My team and I quickly found an empty conference room where we could debrief and investigate. Following client meetings, I almost always tried to arrange a quick "postmortem" for us to openly discuss what went well and where we needed to focus our efforts for improvement. This particular huddle was no fun for any of us.

Turns out, *we were wrong.* The number she questioned was indeed incorrect—we blew it.

I went around the room and literally pointed at every single person and said, "Dave, *you* should have caught this. John, *you* should've caught this. Julio, *you* should have caught this." I continued until every person in the room was on the receiving end of a point. No one was spared. I ended the pointing with a different finger—my thumb. Aimed right back at my chest, I pointed to myself. "And *I* should have caught this. We all failed."

Truth is, if I had been the client in that position, looking at that incorrect number, I'd have reacted similarly. In her mind, seeing an error on one slide meant *every* number on *every* slide was suspect. If we didn't take the time to fact-check something that early in the presentation, why should she be confident we fact-checked and calibrated our numbers at all?

It's probably melodramatic to say that the mistake could have cost us that account. It didn't. However, it *could have*. Clients have ended business relationships over far less. And even though that client stayed with us, our careless mistake certainly didn't help our brand or reputation with her. You can bet she didn't forget this meeting the next time any of us put data in front of her. She also didn't forget how we tried to defend the data; instead of just saying, "Let me double-check that and get back to you," we dug in.

It was clear that we had not done our due diligence before we walked in to that meeting. We all learned a huge lesson from it, the crux of which can be summed up in two words:

Details matter.

Obsessing over the details of your operation and your client's experience enables you to craft the brand you want, in the way you want.

That's why the final WE is simple: WE obsess over details.

Obsessing over the details of your operation and your client's experience enables you to craft the brand you want, in the way you want.

What's the Big Deal?

Throughout the book, I've talked a lot about the importance of "the brand": your personal brand, your team's brand, your company's brand. This kind of branding is what I call "lowercase b" branding. Your personal brand or your team's brand leaves an impression on people, implying a certain level of quality; it's similar to your reputation. And the company's brand is defined by its values and the consistency in which those values are lived out.

"Capital B" branding, on the other hand, is the Brand that represents the whole and makes an experiential impression on the customer. The *Brand* is informed by the combination of all the *brands* that make up the sum of its parts.

When you're driving and you see that bright yellow McDonald's sign, that's the Brand. If you have small children, you surely understand this concept because I'm certain there've been times you've tried to keep them from seeing it. Those golden arches aren't just an *M*. That one letter promises Happy Meals, toys, tasty (not necessarily healthy) food, and full tummies. As a small child, every time I saw those arches, I launched an all-out campaign for a drive-through run, no matter if we were on the way home from another restaurant. That's a powerful Brand—when even a two-year-old gets it.

The "lowercase b" branding is the foundation on which the "capital B" Branding is built—essentially, it makes up the bricks in your wall. For instance, it's no coincidence the experience at a McDonald's in Iowa is the same as the experience in California, which is the same as the experience in Virginia. Without a commitment to uphold its reputation for consistency and quick service, the golden arches wouldn't deliver the powerful experiential impression we all know so well.

Similarly, attention to detail is a critical element of your *personal* brand, which plays a significant role in your *team's* brand, which in turn "ladders up" to the *company* Brand.

How "Obsessed" Are We Talking?

Details can be a polarizing word that elicits very different reactions, depending on who you ask. For some, details are synonymous with "minor," "inconsequential," or "trivial." We've all heard the expression, "Don't sweat the details." For others, the word carries much more weight and importance. This is the group who routinely say something like, "Details make or break the product."

So, when we talk about obsessing over details—what is an appropriate level of obsession? Before we dig deeper into this, I need to make two acknowledgments:

First, I am obsessed with being obsessed about many details that others wouldn't normally obsess about—for example, maintaining consistent font styles and sizes. I even obsess about the placement of staples in collated documents. After all, there was a reason my team at Maximus unapologetically called me "the Shredder." They came up with that nickname—what I consider to be a term of endearment—after seeing me "shred" so many of my team members' presentations. But I'm convinced all the shredding led to an improved product.

And second, although my nickname wouldn't suggest it, I'll clarify: you *can* go too far obsessing over details.

For instance, you've gone overboard obsessing over details if you're spending thirty minutes on a simple task, say typing an email, that would typically take most people three minutes. If you're taking several hours to create a few slides for a staff meeting, you've crossed the line into an unproductive level of obsession.

Obsessing over details is like choosing whether or not to make an investment—you have to evaluate the level of effort or obsession vs. the potential return. If I'm briefing my boss to discuss a small client issue, do I need to take hours to create a slick presentation, or will just a few well-worded bullet points suffice? I'm sure my boss would rather me spend my time on more value-add details and activities than a presentation they will only see for a minute or two.

As a general rule, make sure your obsession with details adds value and is consistent with the priorities on your macro to-do list. Time is a finite resource, so spend it wisely on the work projects that are deserving of your most precious resource.

> Obsessing over details is like choosing whether or not to make an investment—you have to evaluate the level of effort or obsession vs. the potential return.

Still, there's another saying that brings us back to this chapter's main point: "The devil's in the details." I'll spend some time later in this chapter covering how to budget your time to focus on the details that matter most.

So, with a focus on value-add details, here are a few reasons why this WE is so important.

Win by a Nose, Win by a Mile

As a leader, you're a part of a team that's producing a product or service intended to satisfy a consumer's purchasing need—and it's likely you're not the only option the consumer considers when making their purchase. The decision to purchase your product or service is made because there is one or more elements of your product that compels them to buy from you.

So it makes sense that the more obsessed you are with the details involved in producing that product or service, the better the product will be. A laser focus on the details is something that can separate you from your competition, especially if you are in a commodity-based industry.

In the business process outsourcing world, where I've spent so much of my professional time, you don't often win or lose on price because most companies are generally in the same ballpark. You also don't always win or lose on capability either. Because that, too, can be fairly similar from one firm to the next. The details are what compels the buyer to choose you and your product or service.

> It's the little details that give you a competitive edge, differentiating you, your team, your company, and your product from the competition. The details are what compels the buyer to choose you and your product or service.

Show That Special Someone How Much You Care

WE obsess over details because our level of obsession is a direct reflection of our obsessions for our customers' needs. The details are our best and most practical way of showing how much we care about their satisfaction and experience doing business with us. The story from earlier in the chapter about the incorrect number in Brian's presentation is a painful example—if my team couldn't prepare an error-free presentation for our client, why should they trust that any of our work was free from errors?

Simply put, being sloppy with details reflects a lack of care for the customer. That's bad for every aspect of your brand. Likewise, demonstrating attention to detail enhances the best parts of your brand.

> **Demonstrating attention to detail enhances the best parts of your brand.**

Put your consumer hat on for a moment and imagine a purchase that left you over the moon. Was it the product itself, or was it a detail associated with the product? Maybe the company provided something or took care of a detail that might seem minute but was actually really important to you. A seemingly minor experiential detail can make the difference in why you choose one hotel over another, one children's toy over another, or one new car over another.

For instance, I was recently hired by a public school system to deliver a series of Begin With WE keynote addresses. This engagement required me to be in Phoenix for a little over three weeks. The school system booked me in a modest Hilton property for the length of my stay. Since I was going to be in Arizona for a while, I packed a lot. After a few days, my hotel room looked like I'd lived there for months.

Every day, I'd leave the hotel for work and return to a freshly cleaned room—albeit one that retained a little clutter. Then one day, after about a week, my return back to the room was quite different. The hotel cleaning staff didn't just clean the room; they organized my clothes and belongings as well. They didn't just fold some pants and hang some shirts. They hung *every* article of clothing and organized it by color, then by style. Long sleeves were a section, short sleeves another section, and pants and coats were yet another section. They didn't stop there—my chest of drawers had the same level of attention to detail. Socks and undershirts were neatly folded like origami and organized with great care and precision.

Here's the thing: I never asked for any of this—it would have been a little ridiculous if I had. But when I got "home" and opened the closet door, I smiled from ear to ear. The satisfaction I got from the level of care and detail, for the extra effort the hotel crew *chose* to provide, was immense. They delivered a "wow" moment that most other hotels at a similar price point would have never thought to deliver. And this single moment is why I only stay in Hilton properties now.

Attention to detail enables you to go above and beyond to show your customers you care. When the customer can see or feel your focus on the details, especially those that result in an unexpected "wow," the company's Brand is strengthened.

External Affairs

We've already seen how materials shown to clients should be examined with a fine-tooth comb before being presented. However, when it comes to *any* external-facing work product, such as presentations, marketing, or communications collateral, there is only one approach: you must obsess over details. A marketing slick or web-site containing a typo says a lot about the company's Brand. It also begs the question: Since this company doesn't care enough about the details when promoting itself, how much does it care about the production and quality of the product I'm considering buying?

Botching details on ads, packaging, or other forms of communication is a giant red flag to me. I can't get past the lack of attention to detail to consider the product seriously; my prevailing impression is the product was created haphazardly and will not meet my expectations. The company didn't care enough to put its best foot forward; why should I feel differently?

> When it comes to *any* external-facing work product, such as presentations, marketing, or communications collateral, there is only one approach: you must obsess over details.

If you want to see a prime example of what obsessive attention to external-facing detail can do for a company and its Brand, let's revisit Apple. Many people don't even realize it, but Apple's approach to packaging its products is a big reason people love the purchasing experience so much. Videos of "unboxing" of Apple products have millions upon millions of views on YouTube. Consumers have come to expect sleek and simple packaging from Apple. Of course, a lot of time, effort, and obsession over details went into establishing that expectation. Apple even has patents on the design of many of their products' boxes.

In his book, *Inside Apple*, Adam Lashinsky writes, "To fully grasp how seriously Apple executives sweat the small stuff, consider this: For months, a packaging designer was holed up in his room performing the most mundane of tasks—opening boxes."

The designers literally studied and obsessed over the experience of opening a package. Here's the magical result: Apple's customers feel explicitly assured, by the quality of the packaging, the product inside must be equally superior. The packaging provokes an emotional reaction: you're *excited* to open that box and see what's inside.

By contrast, I recently ordered a projector screen, and when it was delivered, right off the bat I noticed several misspelled words on the box. Before I even opened the box, my experience was spoiled and my confidence in the product was ruined. I didn't even open the box because if there was a problem with the screen, I didn't have any reason to think the company would make it right—if they couldn't even proofread the spelling on their own product's package.

Internal Affairs

While the external-facing areas of business represent the "face" that defines the Brand of the company, the behind-the-curtain activity that goes into producing a product or service is just as important.

Someone not familiar with my approach might say, "Why are you spending so much time making sure all the presentation fonts are exactly the same and aligned perfectly? Why are you proofing that all-hands newsletter for the third time?"

Focusing on details isn't a light switch that can be turned on and off depending on the recipient. You can't expect your team to execute flawlessly if you allow careless internal work products. Obsessing over the details of your internal-facing work and your operation is simply a prerequisite for obsessing over the external work that touches your customers.

When you are disconnected from the details of the work being done, it's easy to become disconnected from your customers and your team members—both of which are bad for business.

Sure, there are some instances or contexts where you might let your guard down—for instance, emailing a close friend or confidant. (Obviously, this should be work-related—I'm not giving a pass to send offensive memes around the company. Don't be that idiot.) Your friend or confidant won't be as critical—and if they've earned either of those titles in your life, your personal brand is likely already established with them.

Again, think of this in terms of the brick wall metaphor: you're building your personal brand with everything you produce. Every email is a brick. Every text is a brick.

Shooting off sloppy emails or newsletters to your team communicates details aren't all that important. Consistently showing up late for meetings communicates you aren't obsessed with the details required to efficiently manage others' time. Your approach to details has a ripple effect more far-reaching than you can imagine. You simply cannot lead as a good example while being bad at the details.

> Obsessing over the details of your internal-facing work is simply a prerequisite for obsessing over the external work that touches your customers.

Corporate America's Inattention to Details

I'm not the first author to espouse the benefits of obsessing over details—there are countless companies and leaders that purport to do the same. However, take it from me, many of those same companies and leaders get caught up in matters of volume, and quantity over quality. It's a numbers game, pure and simple; a focus on details can cost more money and slow down the process.

Attention to detail has cost implications that many firms don't want to absorb. Yes, it *can* cost more to slow down the process and obsess over details. Overlooking a few details here or there *will* save money. However, I contend that a great deal of those savings are actually spent in rework costs and customer abrasion. In other words, when companies avoid the costs associated with additional QA steps or additional testing of the product or service, unsightly details are often exposed down the road at a far greater cost—in terms of dollars and Brand reputation. It's a classic case of "pay me now or pay me later."

As firms get bigger, earning the dubious honor of "too big to fail," obsession over details often wanes. The focus ends up almost entirely on growth, revenue, and increased output—not on higher-*quality* output.

And that mentality has led to some horrible mishaps.

The Dangers of Missing Important Details:
Boeing and the 737 MAX 8 Scandal

There are many tragic examples of how overlooking important details resulted in major catastrophes. Another event was recently added to this unfortunate list of examples.

In 2019, airplane manufacturer Boeing came under fire because two 737 MAX 8 planes crashed within months of each other: one flying for Ethiopian Airlines and the other for Lion Air. The two crashes together resulted in the deaths of more than 350 people from over thirty-five countries.

After the second crash, airlines around the world went on high alert because the 737 MAX 8 plane was Boeing's bestselling model at the time, with 387 planes in operation. Many of those planes were grounded by various countries pending investigations of the crashes.

Boeing's official explanation? The planes had a software problem—one they could resolve via an upgrade to a new version of the operating software.

However, in the days after the second crash, increased scrutiny revealed the "software problem" was in fact a serious hardware problem—and the two planes crashed because Boeing made multiple decisions to cut corners and ignore important details in the interest of saving time and money.

When rolling out a new model of plane, airlines must have pilots go through extensive training in simulations of the new models to learn their features and capabilities—a costly but necessary form of QA. Perhaps that's why Boeing specifically designed the 737 MAX 8 to be basically the same plane as the original 737; pilots who had flown 737s would feel familiar with the new model and would likely need less training. There was one major difference between the two models: the MAX 8 had a larger, more fuel-efficient engine.

Unfortunately, in spite of Boeing's intention to make the MAX 8 fly similarly to the 737, the new engines affected the aerodynamics of the old plane design, causing it to fly differently. This "detail" also caused problems with the autopilot systems. As a result, the planes would sometimes nose down after takeoff—which appears to be exactly the case with the doomed Ethiopian and Lion flights.

The bottom line here is the new engines weren't a proper fit, and Boeing knew it. In fact, Boeing designed a cockpit warning light to indicate when the plane's sensors detected a problem during ascent. However, the warning light was an optional add-on to the plane—an $80,000 option.

Not every airline bought it, including Ethiopian Airlines and Lion Air.

Boeing knew there was a danger. And yet, in the interests of protecting its bottom line and saving time, Boeing executives made the decision to move forward and ignore the details that indicated the design could cause problems for pilots and with the functionality of the plane.

The FAA is also to blame. Due to its trust and faith in Boeing and its own lack of funding, the FAA had been allowing Boeing to self-assess and certify the safety of their own planes for years.

In the end, Boeing was charged with a conspiracy to commit fraud against the FAA and was forced to pay $2.5 billion to resolve the charges. This was on top of a $40 billion hit to the company's valuation. The company's reputation and Brand were under tremendous scrutiny. The 737 MAX 8 was grounded for more than a year before being finally recertified to fly again in November 2020. It shouldn't have taken more than 350 deaths to get to this point.

In nearly every crisis where a company was exposed for not doing the right thing, a similar lack of focus on details is almost always uncovered as well. This is why WE 10, "WE obsess over details," is the bookend to WE 1, "WE do the right thing—always." Obsessing over details *is* doing the right thing. And as the Boeing example shows us, to do the right thing, you must obsess over details.

Okay, I'm Ready to Obsess—Tell Me How!

Now that we are aligned on the importance of details to the company, client, and crew, let's look at some practical methods for making this obsession work for you and your team.

Identify the Scope

Remember, it's possible to *over*-obsess. Devoting an inordinate amount of time toward a task that doesn't add an inordinate amount of value is a bad investment of your time. This first strategy is meant to help you be thoughtful about *where* to direct your obsession.

Anytime you're preparing a work product—for example, preparing a presentation or an internal email—assess a couple of important elements and identify the level of obsession warranted.

1. **Who is the audience or recipient?** The answer to this question plays a big role in determining how much time and energy you give. I wholeheartedly believe leaders should aspire for supreme quality for *every* work product—internal and external—with which they are associated. Your emails should always be well written—don't misspell, and don't use bad punctuation and grammar. But obsessing here probably isn't the best use of your precious time. However, a much higher level of obsession is warranted in other contexts. If the work product is *or could be* external-facing in any way, you must commit to an obsession that produces a pristine product

2. **What is the impact if my work product isn't perfect?** This angle helps assess the amount of damage that could be done to your personal brand and that of the company if you let an error slip. A mistake in a presentation for a peer isn't likely to create many problems, whereas an error in a presentation for your boss could damage your personal brand, implying you don't have command over your data—not a good look. The impact of a customer noticing a missed detail, however, could be significant—even leading to losing their business. With that in mind, consider just how "perfect" your output needs to be.

Like so many other topics we've covered, your obsession will be situational. Considering these two questions will help you frame the situation appropriately. In some scenarios, your boss or customer might impose a rigid deadline—essentially dictating the amount of time and obsession to detail you can afford. But more often, it will be entirely up to you to balance the level of the obsession with the time required for your other tasks.

> Balance the level of the obsession with the time required for your other tasks.

Focus on the Trend

Building a Culture of Excellence requires leaders to obsess over trended performance, not one data point in time. While metrics are overwhelmingly important, deny yourself the urge to obsess over the pass/fail of any "moment in time" metric. Let's say that bad customer satisfaction numbers came in for October. As a leader, do I run around the office tearing my hair out, moaning, "We missed it! We failed! We suck!" and other nonsense? No, obviously.

Instead, I need to get people into a room and obsess over the details *underneath* the trended performance. I can't just say, "Get the number up," and poof, it's done. Zeroing in on the details is the only way "fix" what's broken.

> Zeroing in on the details is the only way "fix" what's broken.

The tendency to focus on a single data point is basically the danger of becoming obsessed with a snapshot in time. I'm a fairly active guy, but there are days when I come home and see the fitness tracker on my smartwatch shows only a fraction of the activity of the previous day. I can allow that to get me down, make me worry that I didn't do enough, and vow to make it up the next day...Or I can say, "It's one day. I'm moving on." It's one day. It's not my tombstone. But if it happens again the following day, I need to consider why.

Take note of the data point; then get back to the work of improving the trend.

Understand How the Sausage Is Made

Understanding the details of your people's jobs and how they do those jobs is an area where you should obsess. Besides helping you build trust with your team, this kind of workflow understanding is crucial to properly prioritize the team's efforts.

Take a genuine interest in what your folks are doing. Not as a "Big Brother," hovering over them and micro-managing, but as someone who cares about how they spend their days. I can still recall many hallway conversations, from early in my leadership journey, with leaders who were much more senior in the organization than me. These brief encounters almost always included the question, "How's it going in your shop, Kyle?"

My first thought was always, "Hey, this executive cares about what I'm doing!" It always made me feel excited to answer. Quite often, after my reply, the executive responded in a way that assured they understood my stories. It was obvious when they were close enough to the details of my business to know what the hell I was talking about. I left those conversations energized, eager to tell my team about the encounter: "Hey, one of the big bosses knows who we are and cares about what we're doing!"

Other times, the executive responded in such a way that made it clear they had no clue about my role or what my team did. They didn't know enough to carry on a conversation, challenge me with real questions, or understand my stories. That kind of conversation was always deflating. I was left feeling that executive really didn't give a shit about the people near the front line. If they did, they would've taken the time to ask and learn the details.

Which of these two executives do you want to be?

A good leader *knows*, in some detail, what their people are doing. How do you learn that information? Just ask. Doing skip-level meetings, hosting focus groups, and 1:1 conversations are all perfect opportunities to get closer to the details. You don't have to know everything, but you should be obsessed with learning as much as is practical. It shows you're interested in your people and their success. You can't be anyone's advocate if you don't understand what they're doing.

> A good leader *knows*, in some detail, what their people are doing. It shows you're interested in your people and their success.

Here's a shining example of getting close to the details of your employees' activity. There was a time in Amazon's history when, as part of a training session each year, CEO Jeff Bezos would attend two days of call center training. What better way to be the eyes and ears of the company than sitting next to someone who does it every day—hearing all the good, bad, and ugly details from the consumer?

You don't have to be an expert who knows every detail of your team's work, but building a fundamental base of knowledge and a willingness to understand creates buy-in and connection.

Details vs. Budget

Let's keep it real: our level of obsession with details is directly related to our operating expense budget. If I'm the manager of a Super 8 motel, I might *want* to put 1,000 thread count sheets in every room—but that's not a detail my budget can allow. To some extent, then, the obsession must occur within the confines of your financial reality.

Here's an example. During the first several days of the annual enrollment period for healthcare, enrollment centers have staggering call volume—more than the insurance carriers can possibly handle. For callers to have an ideal service experience without an exaggerated wait time, exponentially more staff would be required during the first week vs. weeks later in the period. However, a few days after open enrollment begins, there is a sharp drop-off in calls. It doesn't make financial sense for an organization to hire and train a fleet of additional call center workers just for those first several days of open enrollment, only to lay them off once there is the drop-off in volume. So instead, most carriers resign themselves to the fact that a certain number of calls will not be answered quickly early in the period. That's a detail in customer care that many insurance providers willfully "eat" due to budget constraints.

It's a harsh reality—and a WE-oriented leader's obsession with details *should* always exceed the level of their budget. But your goal is to maintain a level of obsession *right* at the level that your budget allows. What's more, empower your people to obsess over the details that are free: their treatment of a customer, how they treat one another, and doing the right thing—just to name a few.

These are "budget-neutral" details.

You can't obsess over what *could* be. You can only obsess over what *is*. But there's plenty of room there: the Super 8 manager may not be able to afford 1,000 thread count sheets, but they should fold the 200 thread count sheet with just as much precision. Your budget doesn't dictate your effort, your care for your customers, or your treatment of your people; that's all you.

> A WE-oriented leader's obsession over details *should* always exceed the level of their budget. But your goal is to maintain a level of obsession *right* at the level that your budget allows.

Obsess by Example

All the way back in Chapter 3, I talked about why it is so important that WE lead by example, and here we are again. If you want your people to obsess over details, you have to do it too. And you'll probably have to do it first.

The Amazon example also highlights the importance of leading by example. Jeff Bezos wanted to know the details being provided *to* his company's most important asset (people) *from* the most important voice to Amazon (the customer). He set the example, and leaders from all areas of the company followed. Every year, thousands of managers from all areas of Amazon participate in the same two-day training.

Maybe my approach, becoming the Shredder, was slightly different than Bezos's, but an example was likewise set while I was at Maximus. My team stepped up to a new, heightened appreciation for details. And just as important, they also become "Shredders" in their own right—holding their teams to the same standard.

Only you can determine the appropriate amount of time to dedicate to the details of any given scenario. But you should take this assessment very seriously. Your tendency to obsess over details is an important element to your brand and can matter (a lot) when being considered for new opportunities and career moves.

Another Brick in the Wall

In a 1961 promotional film, iconic architect and designer Charles Eames said, "The details are not the details; they make the product. It will be, in the end, these details that provide service to the customers and give the product its life."

Eames was right—details are not just details. They're not to be scoffed at or minimized. They are critical components that end up building a wall—in the form of a process, a procedure, or a product—that should stand strong. We should be proud to bring our product or service to market, knowing that our obsession with detail ensures its quality.

You can't obsess over a customer's needs without first obsessing over the details behind the curtain. The commitment to a Culture of Excellence where team members care a great deal about details is a prerequisite to ultimate success.

> You can't obsess over a customer's needs without first obsessing over the details behind the curtain. The commitment to a Culture of Excellence where team members care a great deal about details is a prerequisite to ultimate success.

The best products or service in any industry are nothing without the details involved in their creation and delivery. You can't just wake up tomorrow and create some amazing widget the whole world wants. To make it the best widget in the world, you have to obsess over the details required to bring it to life.

It's what WE—the individual, the team, and the company—put into something that makes it great. It's not only about having a pretty wall. It's about ensuring that every brick is placed with perfect precision and care. And that's why WE obsess over details.

THE 10 WEs

WE DO THE RIGHT THING. **ALWAYS.**

WE LEAD BY **EXAMPLE.**

WE SAY WHAT **WE**'RE GOING TO DO. THEN **WE** DO IT.

WE TAKE ACTION. TAKING ACTION AND MAKING A MISTAKE **IS OKAY.** BEING IDLE IS NOT.

WE OWN OUR MISTAKES. **WE**'RE NOT JUDGED BY OUR MISTAKES. **WE**'RE JUDGED BY HOW QUICKLY **WE** REMEDY THEM. AND IF **WE** REPEAT THEM.

WE PICK EACH OTHER **UP.**

WE MEASURE OURSELVES **BY OUTCOMES.** NOT ACTIVITY.

WE CHALLENGE **EACH OTHER.**

WE EMBRACE **CHALLENGE.**

WE OBSESS OVER DETAILS. **DETAILS MATTER. A LOT.**

CONCLUSION

When I created the 10 WEs, I had no idea the lasting impact that would follow. From sitting in that dark hotel room in Kansas to penning this book, I couldn't have imagined how much these principles would change my life and the lives of so many others. I had grown tired of hollow mission statements and inauthentic bosses, and I knew there had to be a better way.

Regardless of industry and regardless of title, most people want to make an impact, want to feel valued, and long to be recognized for their contribution. But as Corporate America has evolved, somehow the focus on the company's greatest asset—its people—has strayed.

But it doesn't have to be this way.

I've always considered it a privilege to lead large organizations and have remained steadfast in my belief that empowering and inspiring others is a leader's obligation. I take pride in being a trustworthy leader who works in the trenches alongside my teams—a leader who is ready and willing to roll up his sleeves and be an advocate for others' development and success.

I've been fortunate to share the 10 WEs with tens of thousands of people across several organizations. Through these experiences, I learned that what I wanted wasn't unique. Not only do most people want to have an impact and be recognized for their contribution, people also yearn to be led with authenticity and transparency. The 10 WEs were my vehicle to establish myself on both of these fronts.

You now have the keys to the same vehicle.

The WEs enable a transition from apathy, to open-mindedness, to absolute conviction. Teammates become less focused on their individual success and instead begin to genuinely care about their impact on, and the success of, their teams and peers.

The *only* way to build a Culture of Excellence is to Begin With WE. There is no substitution for conspicuously stating and then aligning on the principles that fuel the organization. The result of this alignment is a team with an unshakable bond and resolve to embrace (and conquer) the biggest challenges in business.

As the paradigm shifts from "me" to WE, your team will develop a genuine desire to help one another, positioning everyone to succeed. When one functional area performs well but another doesn't, there's recognition that *WE* are not performing well. There's no one person or individual team's success unless the larger "team" is succeeding too. This mindset creates a *real* team rather than an organizational chart. You'll never see a better example of 1+1=3 than a culture committed to WE.

One of the most gratifying results of rolling out the 10 WEs at Maximus came directly from feedback from our biggest client. Three times a year, our clients would participate in an evaluation survey to assess our performance. Within one year of being introduced, the 10 WEs unlocked some of the best evaluation scores Maximus had ever been awarded. We achieved record results in terms of quality, frontline attendance, and customer satisfaction.

But the 10 WEs go well beyond the metrics and survey scores. A culture that begins with WE will change lives. When you show up as an authentic leader, shaping an environment where people pick each other up and inspiring your teams to excel—you experience greater fulfillment in the workplace. That fulfillment will find its way into your personal life as well. In feedback I've gathered from leaders about the 10 WEs, there's always a theme related to the impact the principles have on their home lives. They say the 10 WEs prompted them to be more intentional about quality time with their children and partners. The 10 WEs inspired a growth mindset in their families, with each principle serving as a family value. One person, Julia Willis, Vice President at Maximus, even described the 10 WEs as a code of ethics she uses as a moral framework for her family. And finally, you'll transform individually: when you're confident you're doing the right thing and leading others authentically, you feel differently about the person in the mirror.

It's Time to Begin With WE

It's my goal to help you become the very best leader you can be. And I hope the 10 WEs resonate with you, your team, and your organization. Maybe you found something worthwhile to affirm what you already knew. Or perhaps your eyes have been opened to approaches different than what you've seen during your leadership journey. In either case, you're ready to make a difference in more ways than you ever imagined. Investing in WE, instead of me, gives everyone around you the freedom and resources needed to perform at their highest level.

But I must offer a word of caution:

Culture transformations are like a giant battleship. They can be very effective, but they don't change directions quickly, and they require a lot of coordination. As you begin to implement these principles, take it slow. Getting others on board is a process. You've read the book, and *you* are ready, but your coworkers may not be *there* just yet. So don't expect others to be in the same place you are right off the bat. Like turning the battleship, their adoption of these principles will take time. But as you begin to evangelize and practice the 10 WEs, the ship's wake will be undeniable and followship will ensue.

Encourage your people to read the book and seek to conspicuously align on each of the principles. Make sure you discuss the principles aloud and often, viewing them not only as ideas, but as practical approaches to lean on every day. Your commitment to consistently embrace the 10 WEs is crucial. From time to time, your commitment will be tested. But remember, your actions matter a hell of a lot more than your words. Set a standard, and don't deviate from that standard. If you do err, be transparent and simply admit, "I deviated; I was wrong; I'm owning the mistake."

The benefits will be most obvious within your team first. Capitalize on that momentum by sharing the principles and benefits up the corporate ladder: it's your obligation to bring them to your peers and your leaders. A full embrace of just one team plants the seed for WE growth throughout the entire organization. The larger the organization, the more difficult to spread the message. But ironically, the more you spread the message, the easier it is to implement. The WEs are difficult to refute, and momentum is a critical component of building a Culture of Excellence.

Embrace the Challenge

Writing this book is one of the most difficult challenges I've ever embraced. But I'm convinced sharing the 10 WEs is the right thing and the challenge was worth embracing.

I urge you to do the same—embrace the challenge of making a difference and put these principles into practice. The transformation that unfolds will change how you think about business and your personal impact. The 10 WEs aren't the *only* way to become a better leader, but they're a no-fail roadmap for building and sustaining a Culture of Excellence.

You can have a profoundly positive impact on those around you. You are *already* leading by example—so ensure it's a good one. The *type* of impact you make and the legacy you leave are your choice.

Choose wisely.

Choose courageously.

Choose authentically.

Choose to Begin With WE.

The 10 WEs

1. **WE Do the Right Thing. Always.** This WE is conspicuously first because it sets the standard and expectation for everything that follows. We are not cutting corners. We are going to be proud of the work that we deliver.

2. **WE Lead by Example.** Leaders are always under a microscope, and their behavior and actions will be mirrored. Good or bad, team dynamics will follow the

leader's example—so doing the right thing means leading with integrity and authenticity.

3. **WE Say What WE're Going to Do. Then WE Do It.** Here, we start to establish our brand and our credibility. We must commit to delivering at a certain standard of quality and follow-through because we are only as good as the commitments we keep. The rest is just talk.

4. **WE Take Action. Taking Action and Making a Mistake Is Okay. Being Idle Is Not.** We must never stop searching for any new opportunity to improve and be more effective. In both professional development and our own personal growth, taking action puts us in a position to reach new heights and be better than we were yesterday. When we see an opportunity to advance the team, we must act. Not taking action means becoming stagnant—and that's when you get lapped.

5. **WE Own Our Mistakes. WE're Not Judged by Our Mistakes. WE're judged by How Quickly WE Remedy Them. And if WE Repeat Them.** Mistakes are a natural component of the evolutionary process. There is no shame in a mistake, but there must be ownership. Owning mistakes avoids wasted time spent trying to assign blame, allowing for expedient resolution and a more objective approach to guarding against a repeat.

6. **WE Pick Each Other Up.** We must foster an environment in which no one person is more important or better than the next. We all need help from time to time, and it's everyone's responsibility to pick up our teams and coworkers when needed. Doing so creates a connected tribe with a caring sense of community.

7. **WE Measure Ourselves by Outcomes. Not Activity.** Measuring ourselves by activity provides an illusion of progress and gets us nowhere. We are paid for outcomes; that's what the real world judges us by. We must ensure that all activity is directly linked to outcomes.

8. **WE Challenge Each Other. Diplomatically.** Whether from internal or external sources, challenge is fuel for the continuous improvement engine. We must hold each other to high standards, challenging one another when we see complacency or an opportunity to improve. Mediocrity and the status quo thrive in a culture void of challenge.

9. **WE Embrace Challenge.** Challenges are a constant. If we deny their existence, we get lapped and replaced. We must instead view each challenge as an opportunity for personal *and* professional growth. We set aside ego and recognize challenges aren't personal—the only way to objectively view and overcome the situation.

10. **WE Obsess Over Details. Details Matter. A Lot.** Details are not just "details" but "Details." Details are essential elements of every process and our differentiator for success. Our fixation on every single detail—big, small, and everything in between—matters a whole hell of a lot. Our personal brand and the brand of our company depend on the executing of the details.

About the Author

Kyle McDowell is a former senior executive with a track record of delivering unprecedented results, leading thousands of employees for the likes of industry giants CVS Health, Maximus, United Health Group (Optum), and Bank of America.

McDowell has a passion for developing truly authentic and courageous leaders, as well as an unwavering belief there's a better way to lead and thrive in Corporate America. This compelled him to create The 10 WEs, his guiding principles for building and sustaining a Culture of Excellence.

After successfully weaving The 10 WEs into the cultural fabric of massive organizations, McDowell left Corporate America to write *Begin With WE* and launch Kyle McDowell Inc., a global coaching, consulting, and speaking firm dedicated to improving organizational effectiveness by transforming **bosses** into **leaders**.

McDowell's leadership has been featured in the *Wall Street Journal*, the *Boston Herald*, and the *Burlington Free Press*. He holds an MBA from the Kellogg School of Management at Northwestern University.

KyleMcDowellInc.com
Twitter: *@kylemcdowellinc*
Instagram: *@kylemcdowellinc*